Compelled by the Cross

J. Terry Young

BROADMAN PRESS
Nashville, Tennessee

Dedicated to my Mother
Mildred Thiel Young,
Who led me to the cross
and the living Savior

© Copyright 1980 • Broadman Press.

4252-82

ISBN: 0-8054-5282-6

Dewey Decimal Classification: 232.963

Subject heading: JESUS CHRIST—CRUCIFIXION

Library of Congress Catalog Card Number: 80-66768

Printed in the United States of America

Contents

Contents

Introduction

Years ago I was helping photograph several groups of people in a church auditorium. In the dim light it was a little difficult to focus the camera properly since people were scattered across the front of the auditorium. It was hard to find a person or an object in the right place for the center of focus. Finally someone suggested, "Focus on the cross, and everything will come out all right."

That is the message of this book. Keep the cross in perspective and everything will come out all right. The cross stands at the heart of the Christian faith. Everything else in Christianity derives its meaning from its relation to the cross of Jesus Christ.

Christianity does not worship a dead Christ, still hanging on the cross. But Christianity does look up to a resurrected Savior who achieved victory over sin and death by means of the cross. The cross, then, has become the symbol of the Christian faith.

There are many dimensions to the cross. The cross stands for what Jesus did in providing salvation for lost sinners. It stands for the missionary imperative at the heart of Christian faith. It symbolizes the eternal love of God. It signifies the solemn responsibilities of the Christian life. No one has ever fully understood all the implications of the cross. Its full meaning, and all of its implications, are always out ahead of us.

The cross is like a beautiful diamond. A diamond slowly rotated under bright light presents the viewer with an endless array of dazzling beauty. Each different viewing angle presents a vivid new scene.

The cross is like that. It can be viewed from many different perspectives, and each new angle affords a fresh, new insight into its meaning from several different perspectives.

6

I am grateful to Mrs. Teresa Bishop Crawford for typing the preliminary and final drafts of the manuscript. Her capable assistance has made the preparation of this book easier and more enjoyable than it might otherwise have been.

1
Why the Cross?

Stand in the crowded walkways of a busy shopping mall and ask a single question of the people who mill about window shopping. Ask, "Why the cross—why did Jesus Christ die on the cross?" You will receive a surprising variety of answers and reactions to that simple question.

Some will simply shrug their shoulders, with a quizzical look on their faces, and reply, "I don't know." They are superficially aware that the cross is associated with the church and has some religious significance, but they are scarcely aware that Jesus died on a cross. They have no idea why he died or what his death means.

Keep on asking, "Why the cross?" The answers will continue to come. Some will tell you that the cross is an isolated event in history and has no further meaning for today. But such an answer demands explanation. If you press for an explanation, someone will explain that the death of Jesus on the cross was only the natural result of a life as pure as his being lived in such a sinful world as this. His goodness was so evident that he was a living condemnation of the wickedness that infected all those about him. The righteousness of both his teaching and his example was like a searchlight suddenly turned on wicked men caught in the act of their rebelliousness.

The Bible itself affirms the opposition of evil men to the light that was shining in Jesus. "And this is the judgment, that the light has come into the world, and men love the darkness rather than light, because their deeds were evil. For every one who does evil hates the light, and does not come to the light, lest his deeds should be exposed" (John 3:19-20). Indeed, so intense was the opposition of evil men to the light that was in Jesus that it was not long until they plotted his death.

In this sense the cross was an isolated event in history, rooted in the tragic circumstances of that particular time. The death of Jesus was the result of a life as pure as his being lived in a sinful world. An example of what happened to Jesus can be seen in our own day. Victor Riesel, a labor columnist for the news media, was exposing racketeering practices in certain labor unions. Those who feared the searchlight of his exposés hired thugs who stood in a darkened alley one evening and threw acid in Victor Riesel's face as he passed. Riesel was disfigured and blinded. He was a victim of the very evil he was trying to expose.

Another person might explain that he views the cross as an isolated event without significance for us today because it was simply one more sad example of the miscarriage of justice in an evil world. No credible charge was ever made against Jesus. Witnesses had to be bribed to bring any charges at all against Jesus. The case against him was so ridiculous that Jesus did not once speak a word in self-defense. The six trials held in rapid succession were all illegal, even by the standards of that day. Finally, a cowering, indecisive governor allowed him to be executed even though he was convinced of his innocence. His death was a tragic miscarriage of justice and, some would say, ought to be viewed as an isolated event of history that has no significance for us in our day.

Jesus' death on the cross could also be seen as the result of the religious jealousy of the Jewish establishment of his day. As a popular young preacher with a fresh message, Jesus was attracting a great deal of attention. Indeed, he was turning attention from the Temple establishment and the institutional synagogues to the message that he was speaking. And the message that he was speaking was often a scathing denunciation of the legalism of the Pharisees and a call for something better than the Jewish system of that day could produce. Jesus was on a collision course with the Jewish establishment and the Jews were extremely jealous of him because he was taking their crowds. In fact, they soon came to realize that Jesus was a direct threat to their system and began to plot his downfall. They tried to discredit him in the eyes of the people with tricky questions but Jesus each time succeeded in turning the tables on his interrogators and embarrassing the Jewish establishment. As a last resort they plotted his death and succeeded in silencing him when he was finally nailed to a cross in a semiofficial riot.

So, some would say that his death on the cross has to be seen as an isolated event in history, explained by the circumstances of the times.

All of this may be true; we may be able to explain his death in terms of the circumstances of the day in which he lived. But, this does not explain why Jesus seemed to point his whole life toward the cross. He viewed the cross as the crowning achievement of his life, the very purpose for which he had come into the world. In messianic prophecy it was said of Jesus, "Therefore I have set my face like a flint" (Isa. 50:7). He would not be deterred from the suffering and death to which he committed himself. When he first told his disciples that he must die, Peter rebuked him and tried to turn his thoughts away from such a foreboding future. But Jesus, in turn, rebuked Peter, whom he had praised only moments before, saying, "Get behind me, Satan! You are a hindrance to me; for you are not on the side of God, but of men" (Matt. 16:23).

Jesus was not looking for an alternative to the cross, or an escape from the cross. The cross, though it may have had historical explanation, had a far larger significance for Jesus than screaming mobs, crooked courts, and jealous, wicked men trying to protect themselves. Jesus was determined to go to the cross. It was the high point of his life. It was what he had come to do. But why?

Why the cross? We must continue asking the question. Someone will answer that the cross was God's way of defeating the evil of this world. At the beginning of human history evil infected God's perfect creation, tempting Adam and Eve to rebel against God through a selfish choice of the forbidden fruit in the Garden of Eden. It is pointless to speculate about the origin of evil—the tempter who led Adam and Eve astray. It is terribly important, however, to see that from the time of Adam's sin God was moving toward a showdown with sin, with the evil that infected his creation. Even in the Garden of Eden, God addressed the tempter, saying, "I will put enmity between you and the woman,/and between your seed and her seed;/he shall bruise your head,/and you shall bruise his heel" (Gen. 3:15). From the Old Testament perspective, it is far from clear what this veiled reference means; but as we look back from the New Testament perspective, it becomes clear that God was announcing from the beginning that he would ultimately destroy the power of evil in the world.

The cross is the sign of God's struggle with the power of evil. It is the instrument that he used in breaking sin's power. Jesus himself saw his death as a victory, not a defeat, for God. Shortly before his death, Jesus told his disciples, "I have overcome the world" (John 16:33). In the same spirit, Jesus had declared a little earlier, "Now is the judgment of this world, now shall the ruler of this world be cast out; and I, when I am lifted up from the earth, will draw all men to myself" (John 12:31-32). The cross of Jesus Christ spelled the defeat of Satan. It was God's victory over evil—and it was won through the death of Jesus Christ upon the cross.

Some will ask, however, how the death of Jesus was a victory for God. With the Son of God hanging upon a cross in pitiful death, it would appear that God had lost a battle rather than won one. But take a closer look. Victory is sometimes costly. Consider an example.

A family was spending a quiet evening at home watching television. They thought they heard a noise in another part of the house. One of them went to see what it was. In a moment she returned, forced back into the room by a big, burly man brandishing an ugly-looking revolver. They immediately recognized him as an escapee from a nearby hospital for the criminally insane. They knew from the newscast they had heard only a little earlier that he was considered extremely dangerous.

Through the long hours of the night, the crazed gunman held the terrified family captive, threatening to kill first one and then another of them. At times he waved the gun right in their faces, sometimes cocking it, holding a nervous finger on the trigger.

The next morning, as the neighborhood began to stir, neighbors noticed that the husband did not leave for work as usual. They also noticed, a little later, that the children did not leave for school. A kindly neighbor, thinking that perhaps there was illness in the family, came from next door to see if something was wrong. As she approached the front door she could see what was happening through the picture window in the living room. She called police officers who came quickly and surrounded the house. However, there was very little that they could do, for any move that they might make would almost certainly have meant death for one or more of the members of the family.

The tense drama wore on through long hours of the day. Seemingly, it was a stalemate that defied solution. Late in the day the father in the family sensed that the gunman was growing more weary and nervous. He sensed that if something were not done soon the gunman might very well kill some of them.

In desperation, the father pointed to a window and shouted, "Look!" to distract the attention of the gunman. For a brief moment the gunman did look toward the window, and in that brief instant the father lunged at him, struggling for the gun. In the life-and-death struggle, the gun went off and killed the valiant father who was trying to save his family from harm.

The father did save his family from harm, even though it was at a great price—his own life. But it was a sacrifice he was willing to make if it were the only way that he could set his family free and protect them from harm at the hands of a crazed killer. That noble father won the victory, but at a terrible cost.

In the few moments of struggle on the floor for the possession of the gun, law officers had just enough time to kick in the front door, dash into the room, and seize the gunman before he could do further harm to his captives.

This is an illustration in miniature of what happened on the cross. Jesus Christ saw humanity held captive by death and sin. He stepped in to take upon himself all of the power of sin and death. He conquered sin in his sinless life and took upon himself all of the suffering that death could offer. Indeed, he died a cruel death, but in so doing he broke the power of death. For death could not hold him. The grave had to give up its spoils as Jesus was resurrected three days later.

The cross was the sign of the cosmic struggle of God to break the power of sin and death that had invaded his world. In truth, he won the victory in that cosmic struggle to overcome the alien enemy at work in his world, but the victory that God won came at a very high price. God himself had entered the stream of human history in the person of his Son, Jesus Christ, to struggle with the forces that were destroying the lives of men. As Gustaf Aulen puts it in his little book *Christus Victor,* Christ was the victor on the cross, not the victim.

It was for this reason that Jesus saw the cross as the crowning achievement of his life. He won the victory for man that man could not win for himself. The cross was God defeating the powers of evil that were operative in his world.

God could have wiped the face of the earth clean in sweeping judgment anytime he wanted to. That had already been demonstrated in the Flood which came as God's judgment on the wickedness of Noah's day. The cross was more than God defeating sin and Satan.

Ask again, why the cross? Someone will suggest that the cross was God's action in righteously providing atonement for the sin of man. This was God's way of enduring the penalty for sin for man. God was allowing his Son, Jesus Christ, to become a substitute for man in bearing the consequences of sin in death on the cross.

In defying his Creator, humanity, through sin, had placed itself under the penalty of death for sin. In a moral universe, under the sovereign lordship of a holy and righteous God, sin is a serious affront to God and cannot be lightly dismissed. In fact, it was very early that God warned man that sin brings death, saying, "The soul that sins shall die" (Ezek. 18:4). Indeed, the teaching that sin brings death goes all the way back to God's warning to Adam and Eve in the Garden of Eden when he warned them that sinning would bring death. The cross was God's dramatic way of proclaiming man's forgiveness, man's release from the penalty of his sin.

It was not enough for God simply to declare man forgiven. The forgiveness needed to be declared in a manner that emphasized the seriousness of man's sin, and that would stress the costliness of his forgiveness. The forgiveness needed to be declared in a way that would make perfectly clear in a dramatic demonstration, that God had taken on himself the results of mankind's sin, so that humanity might go free in salvation.

The cross was one way for God to show that sin is terribly serious and that forgiveness is no easy, cheap matter. Even at the human level, society finds it necessary to punish crime as a means of demonstrating the seriousness of crime in man's society. The fine exacted when one runs a red light and the jail term imposed when he robs a bank are meant not only to inflict punishment on the guilty—which they deserve—but are also meant to serve as a warning to others that lawlessness, of whatever sort, is serious and brings penalty.

On the spiritual level, the cross was God's way of showing his displeasure with sin, his righteous opposition to sin, of whatever sort. It was his means of declaring his own respect for right and wrong.

God wanted to free man from the just penalty of his sin, but he wanted to do it in a way that would underscore both the opposition of God to sin and the costliness of salvation. The cross was God's way of paying the price, so to speak, of man's release from the penalty of his sin. Do not misunderstand the price that Jesus paid for our redemption. It was not a bookkeeping transaction. It was the cost of God stooping to our level to free us. When Jesus humbled himself to live as one of us in human form, it cost him a tremendous price to leave behind the glory that rightfully was his. It cost him to submit meekly to the suffering and shame that we poured upon him. It cost him to die on the cross as the final act of sacrifice in the Old Testament sacrificial system which proclaimed the saving grace of God.

The cross was God's way of stepping into the predicament of humankind and taking his place so man might be freed from his peril in the results of his sin. Peter said that Jesus "himself bore our sins in his body on the tree, that we might die to sin and live to righteousness. By his wounds you have been healed" (1 Pet. 2:24). The cross was God's way, then, of announcing our forgiveness, while at the same time fully emphasizing the infinite seriousness of our sins and the costliness of our redemption.

Some may have a difficult time relating the cross to the loving forgiveness of God. Perhaps an illustration at the human level may make a little clearer how love and righteousness united in the cross of Jesus Christ to provide a righteous way of forgiving us. A certain judge was known in his local community for his sternness in "throwing the book" at offenders who were convicted in his courtroom. He sought to make each case an example which would speak loudly and clearly against lawlessness. Many observers of the court wondered if there was any compassion in the judge. In fact, many thought there was not because of the sternness of the sentences he passed out.

However, there came a day when many thought they would see a different side to the judge. The accused man who stood before the bench was a boyhood chum of the judge. After the arguments in the case had been heard, the judge asked the defendant if he had any personal remarks to make before the court rendered its verdict. The man made an eloquent and tearful plea to the judge for mercy. He reminded the judge that they had been friends for a long time. He reminded the judge that he really had not had much of a chance in life, having come from a broken home on the wrong side of the tracks where a succession of alcoholic stepfathers had beaten and abused him. People in the courtroom were moved by the pathetic story the man was telling in self-defense as he pleaded for mercy.

When his plea was ended, the judge thought in silence for a few moments. Then he sternly announced, "As the judge of this court I have no alternative but to find you guilty as charged and to sentence you to one year in jail or a fine of $1,000." The defendant was shocked. Indeed, all in the courtroom seemed stunned at the apparently harsh action of the judge. However, as the people sat in stunned silence, and the defendant stood visibly shaken, the judge arose from behind the bench. He quickly came to the side of his friend from boyhood days, slipped his arm around his shoulder, and said quietly, "As the judge of this court I have no alternative but to fine you the limit of the law for your crime, *but as your friend I will pay the fine myself.*" With that he reached into his inside coat pocket, took out his checkbook, and wrote out his own personal check to pay the fine of his unfortunate friend.

In a limited way, this is a human illustration of a great, divine truth. This is a miniature picture of what God was doing through the death of Jesus Christ upon the cross. He was dramatically demonstrating his displeasure with sin and, at the same time, taking the consequences of our sins upon himself. Speaking of this action of God through Jesus Christ, Paul said, "For our sake he made him to be sin who knew no sin, so that in him we might become the righteousness of God" (2 Cor. 5:21).

Still, we have not plumbed the depths of the meaning of the cross. God did not have to save man. He did not have to forgive man. He did not have to take upon himself the consequences of our sin. He could have left us in our predicament. He could have left us to suffer the consequences of our rebellion against him. After all, he had warned us of the consequences of our sin. He could well have punished us for our sins. We deserved his punishment. Why, then, the cross? Is there something more to the cross? Perhaps we should keep on asking.

Why the cross? Someone will suggest that the cross was the result of the love of God. Jesus died on the cross as the supreme revelation of God's love to us. The key verse in all of the Scriptures is John 3:16, "For God so loved the world that he gave his only Son, that whoever believes in him should not perish but have everlasting life." The cross came as the supreme act of God's love. It was the highest possible manifestation of the love of God for sinful, perishing men.

A loving heavenly Father formed man from the dust of the ground at the beginning of the world and placed him in a garden paradise. Adam was created in God's own image and had almost unbelievable possibilities before him. But Adam blew it! He quickly succumbed to temptation. He asserted himself in sinful selfishness. He rebelled against God, disobeying the commandment that God had evidently made quite plain to him. And man subjected himself to the judgment of God. He placed himself under the wrath of God.

Do not misunderstand the wrath of God. God's wrath is not a fit of anger that he has against man. It's not even a fit of anger that he has against a rebel who has dared to defy the Almighty. The wrath of God is what man experiences when he turns his back on the love of God. The wrath of God is the reverse side of God's love. It is how man experiences God's outreach to him when he is resisting every advance of God, rebelling against him. The wrath of God is the inevitable consequence of refusing the blessing of God. It is not a disposition of ill will on the part of God, not even toward a sinner in defiance of his creator.

But the experience of the wrath of God—the desolation that

one brings on himself by rejecting the loving advances of God—is an awesome reality. Man breaks himself on the eternal love of God. When man chooses to reject God and assert himself in ultimate selfishness, he subjects himself to dire consequences. These are tragic consequences in both time and eternity. Man undoes himself in this life by his rebellion against God. He brings upon himself all kinds of suffering. He fails to become what he could have been. But even worse, he brings on himself eternal judgment for his sin against his righteous Creator.

The wrath of God is not a negative disposition on the part of God towards a sinner. It is his refusal to alter his demand for righteousness. It is his refusal to alter his own character. It is his refusal to compromise with man. The wrath of God, properly understood, is the consequence of man's own action, not that of God. Man throws himself into the open, grinding machinery of sin and evil and suffers the consequences. The wrath of God is not God inflicting punishment upon the sinner. It is the sinner refusing to take God seriously.

The idea that God takes delight in punishing the sinner has no basis in the Bible. God is not some kind of celestial despot, acting with arbitrary caprice, gleefully inflicting punishment on all that he can. That kind of a caricature of God has more in common with something out of Dante than with Scripture.

The biblical picture of God is one that gives us a God who is brokenhearted over the sinful rebelliousness of his children. He has no pleasure in the suffering or death of any. In fact, the exact opposite is true. The biblical picture of God shows him grieved over men who are suffering and perishing in the tragic results of their sins. He is actively at work trying to turn men from their sins to accept his forgiveness and regenerative grace. Even the Old Testament prophets of judgment picture the brokenhearted God longing for the salvation of his people. "As I live, says the Lord God, I have no pleasure in the death of the wicked, but that the wicked turn from his way and live, turn back, turn back from your evil ways; for why will you die, O house of Israel?" (Ezek. 33:11).

The cross of Jesus Christ was the supreme revelation of God's love for man. It was his way of stepping into the human situation—throwing himself into the open, grinding machinery of sin and death in order to break its power and offer an alternative to man. The apostle Paul put it graphically, saying, "God shows his love for us in that while we were yet sinners Christ died for us" (Rom. 5:8). Even at the very time we were at war with God, God was manifesting his love for us by stepping in under the judgment that we were bringing upon ourselves.

How far is this picture from that of a God waiting for an opportunity to inflict punishment upon the sinner. Here is a God who is stepping into the very destruction that we were wreaking upon ourselves and taking the full consequences upon himself in order that we might go free. On the cross God was stepping into our situation in order that we might yet attain the life that God has planned for us from the beginning. The cross, then, is the supreme example of the love of God for us, the highest possible revelation of the love of God. Jesus himself said, "Greater love has no man than this, that a man lay down his life for his friends" (John 15:13).

The cross was the dramatic demonstration of God's love for us. Here he took on himself the consequences of our sin simply because he loved us. Perhaps that kind of love is illustrated at the human level by the story of a man who gave himself in a heroic action to save the life of a longtime friend. The two men were working on a construction site one day. One of them glanced upward at a load of steel beams being moved by a giant crane. Suddenly, the load shifted and the beams started to fall. In the noise of the construction site it was impossible to shout a warning, and there really wasn't time anyway. Instantly he lunged at his friend, sending him sprawling, but safely out from under the crashing steel girders. However, in his frantic effort to save his friend's life, he fell under the crashing beams himself. Perhaps this is a simple, human illustration of a great divine truth: God loves us so much that he threw himself into the consequences of our sin—*death*—and took its worst upon himself to demonstrate his love for us. He gave his Son as a substitute for us. By his death our salvation is made possible.

But keep on asking, Why the cross? To say that the cross was the supreme revelation of the love of God for us is true, but it sounds a bit distant and abstract. That was something that happened nearly two thousand years ago and it affects all who receive the message of the crucified Savior. Isn't there more to the cross than that? Doesn't it come closer home than that? Isn't it more than a general principle? Isn't it more specific and personal?

The deepest significance of the cross came home to me one day in a most unexpected way, in a way that I have not forgotten in twenty-five years or more. It was during a chapel service while I was a seminary student. A youth group from a church several hundred miles away were giving a drama set in biblical times. I have long since forgotten the particular church from which the youth had come and the name of the play that they performed. But I shall never forget the message that came through to me.

As I remember it, the play opened with the setting in the living room of a carpenter's home in Jerusalem, during the time of the earthly life of Jesus. The family—husband and wife, and their two children—were enjoying a quiet evening together, discussing the events of the day. The mother in the family reported that when she was in the marketplace that day she had seen a notice posted by the Roman government inviting carpenters to submit model crosses and a bid for the contract to supply crosses for the local executions. She began to urge, and finally to nag, her husband to submit a bid for the contract. She had all kinds of ideas how they could use the extra money. It would provide many of the things she thought they needed.

However, the husband was not the least interested in making crosses for executions. He was a proud craftsman. He liked to think of his work bringing happiness and joy to people. He wanted to enrich life through his work, not provide an instrument of death. Nevertheless, after considerable nagging from his wife, he reluctantly gave in and agreed to submit a model cross and a bid for the contract. However, it was obvious that he hoped he would not get the contract.

As the play goes on the little boy in the family, some ten or twelve years old, works in the carpenter shop, helping his father. He is proud of the work he is doing, learning the carpentry trade. Near the end of the play the little boy comes running into the house, crying as though his heart were breaking. The father and mother gather round him, asking what in the world has him so upset. The little lad sobs that he has just seen a mob taking Jesus out to be crucified. The family shares in the sorrow that has over-whelmed the little boy. They have heard Jesus teach and preach, and they have been greatly impressed by him. However, the father cannot really understand why his son is so upset at the thought of Jesus being crucified. "You have seen other prophets crucified! Why are you so upset this time?"

"Daddy, you don't understand," sobbed the little boy, all the harder. "They are going to crucify Jesus on the cross that we made right here in our shop!"

"Son, you don't know that! There were many crosses made at the same time that we made ours."

"But, Daddy, I do know that it was the cross we made!"

"How do you know, Son?"

"Do you remember when the man came to talk to you about new cabinets for his kitchen last week? While you were outside talking to him, I was looking at the cross that we were making. It was just about finished, and I was so proud of the work that I had done. I thought that I would do as the great artists do and sign my name on it somewhere.

"Daddy, when Jesus was carrying that big heavy cross, he was having a hard time with it. He was all bruised and bleeding from the things they had done to him. Daddy, he fell under the weight of the cross. Daddy, he fell right in front of me—and when he fell I could see that my name was on the cross that he was carrying!"

"My name was on that cross!" There it was, like a bolt out of the blue. Suddenly, the full meaning of the cross came home to me.

My name was on that cross!

2
The Cross in Our Midst

The cross took on a new dimension of meaning for me when I saw it in what may very well be the world's largest painting. I saw it in a different perspective, a perspective that forced me to imagine the cross as though it were happening in my own time, in my own town. Somehow, the faces on the canvas made me think of their counterparts in my day.

The unusual painting that I saw was done by the Polish artist Jan Styka. Styka, who took part of his inspiration from the famed musician Paderewski, gave his interpretation of Jesus and his cross on a giant canvas. His picture was so large that it had to be done in a warehouse. The picture is 45 feet high by 195 feet long. In 1900 the picture was brought to America for display at the St. Louis Exposition, but there really was no place large enough to show it properly. After that it lay neglected in a warehouse for many years, too large to display anywhere. Then it was discovered by an American Christian businessman. Hubert Eaton, who was the founder of the famed Forest Lawn Memorial Park in Glendale, California, thought that it was such a powerful rendition of the scene of Jesus and his cross that he bought it. He built a special building to house it on the grounds of the Forest Lawn Memorial Park in Glendale. Now it is on display to the public and thousands of people have come to view it and hear the dramatic interpretation of the scene on the canvas. The picture is so overwhelming in size as well as content that it takes quite awhile with a careful narration for one to take it all in.

Styka has painted the crucifixion scene, not with Jesus hanging on the cross near death. He pictures Jesus, near the left side of the canvas, standing beside the cross in the moments before he was nailed to it. The guards are preparing to crucify him. Across the canvas, all the way to the right side, is a sea of people, streaming

20

out of the city of Jerusalem. They are making their way to the hill of Golgotha to watch the execution of Jesus. Styka has given a fantastic portrayal of the scene about the cross. One can sit for hours looking at the people Styka has carefully painted into the gigantic scene. They are young. They are old. They are poor. They are rich. Some are utterly happy. Some are seriously downcast. Others are indifferent looking, just caught up in the milling mob in something of a carnival atmosphere.

As I watched the faces of the various people around the cross in Styka's painting, I found myself wondering what would the scene be if Jesus were to be crucified today in the parking lot of a great shopping center. What kind of folk might we see crowding about the cross? I think I saw them in Styka's picture of Calvary. Human nature is pretty much the same today as it was when Jesus died nearly two thousand years ago. Turn your imagination loose and see if you can visualize the scene.

You can't imagine the scene of the crucifixion without visualizing the lonely figure of Jesus. Styka pictured him standing alone, serene, tinged with a look of compassion and pity for the milling crowd which has been shouting for his death. Though Styka painted him near the left side of the canvas, one's attention is immediately drawn to him as the central figure. And so he is. He may be a pathetic looking figure as he is about to be nailed to the cross, but he is certainly the world's central figure, the central figure in the world's most important event.

As you see him standing by that cross, and as you think back upon who he is, what kind of life he has lived, and what he came to do, he is certainly the world's most misunderstood man. He came to bring a message of love and now is dying as a victim of mindless jealousy and anger, rejected and condemned by the very people he came to help. He has lived a life of purity and righteousness—the only person who ever lived without sin—and now he is about to die a common criminal's death. He died a paradoxical death. His death opened the door of life—eternal life—to many. He died that others might live.

There was a variegated sort of humanity surrounding that cross. You can pick out the different kinds of people just by studying the faces in the crowd. Some of them are obviously just curious people who came along with the crowd just to see what was going on. They may very well account for the carnival-like atmosphere. They just came along for a good time.

Some people have a morbid sense of curiosity. No matter what is going on they just have to see the inside of it. I once knew a man who had the most morbid sense of curiosity I have ever heard about. He was an influential man whose name could get him on the inside of many things where you or I could not go. And he often went to satisfy his strange sense of curiosity. For instance, he had a strange compulsion to see dead bodies. Especially the bodies of those who had died violent, maiming deaths. His connections could get him inside many morgues and embalming rooms. Any time he heard of someone being mutilated in a terrible wreck, or of someone who had committed suicide in a leap from a tall building, he went as soon as possible to view the grotesquely mutilated body. And he took some kind of special delight in these gory scenes.

Some who stood about the cross were of that sort. It really made no difference to them what was taking place there. It really didn't matter that an innocent man was dying—or that the Son of God was dying in order to bring lost men out of their sins. They had simply come along for the show. A public execution was good for several hours of entertainment as the poor victim was wracked by pain and life slowly faded from his suffering body. Men who ought to have been stricken in conscience, humbled in shame, and filled with utter despair and sorrow simply stood in morbid curiosity to watch a free show.

There were also hardened men there. Their hearts were icy cold and as hard as nails. Seemingly, there wasn't anything that could really move them to sympathy or compassion. Some of them had been shouting for the death of Jesus. It was easier to bring about the execution of Jesus than to yield to his demands for repentance. After all, if Jesus kept on in his demands for a religion that really made a difference in people's lives, they would have to change themselves and their comfortable old system of easy religion that was only skin-deep in its superficiality. Thus, when they saw Jesus about to be nailed to the cross, they rejoiced and uttered a sigh of relief.

It made no difference to them that the blackest deed of all time was being perpetrated before them, even because of them. Many of these hardened people were not the least bit moved by what was taking place that day, and some of them actually took satisfaction in some sort of sweet revenge. Heaven itself was being dragged through the slime of earth's sin and the very Son of God was being crucified in a horrible death, and they viewed it all without so much as a tear. Some even gloated in satisfaction. What kind of animals were these who could view the cross with dry eyes?

Hard, vicious hearts like this are hard to understand. I think I saw the ultimate example of such hardheartedness one afternoon at the scene of a tragic accident. I was doing some pastoral visitation in the middle of the afternoon. About a block ahead of me I saw a school bus sitting diagonally in the intersection. When I got to the intersection, I saw that I could ease around the end of the bus by carefully maneuvering. I slowly started around the end of the bus, not knowing what had happened, or why the bus was sitting as it was in the intersection. Just as I pulled around the front of the bus I saw a scene that I shall never forget. Alongside the bus was the horribly crushed body of a young woman who had been driving a car which was struck by the bus. The upper part of her body had been run over by the dual wheels on the back of the bus.

I was about the first to come upon the scene. I got out of my car and proceeded to direct traffic until police officers came to take charge, lest some other tragedy happen there. When I could, I asked the driver of the school bus what had happened. I was dumbstruck by her answer. She pointed to the pool of blood and mangled flesh on the pavement and said, "That old fool ran through the stop sign and she got what she deserved." My blood nearly turned to ice water. I fought back tears as I wondered just how hardhearted one can get. There was a young mother, sole support for three little children, smeared over the pavement in a busy intersection. And the one who had inadvertently killed her was unmoved by it all except for anger in being delayed in completing her bus route. That's how hardhearted some were who stood around the cross of Jesus.

There were others who were simply indifferent. They found no particular joy in what was taking place. They weren't even particularly curious. They were really rather oblivious to what was happening. They were just there. There are always folk like that. They don't quite know what is going on. They are not very much concerned about anything. I saw a good number of them on the street corner where the young mother was killed in the bus accident. Quite a crowd gathered as we waited for the police, an ambulance, and wreckers. It was a busy intersection.

A passing ice-cream vendor stopped—he saw a potential bonanza in the gathering. It sort of turned my stomach to see so many in the crowd standing around licking popsicles and ice cream bars while they were watching workmen scoop up the broken body of the poor woman killed there just a little earlier. For the most part they were oblivious to the sad scene they were watching. They had no way of knowing that there were three little children at home who were now both fatherless and motherless. It was not until I saw it in the newspapers the next day that I caught the full impact of that tragedy. However, just watching the crushed form of a fellow human being, no matter what the larger circumstances, was a heartbreaking experience for me. I not only didn't want an ice cream bar, I didn't even want dinner that night. I couldn't forget the tragedy of the scene I had witnessed. But some were so indifferent to the human tragedy before them, they could make wisecracks and lick popsicles.

Some around the cross that day were just that indifferent. They really didn't know what was going on. And they really didn't care. They were there simply because there was nothing better to do. They watched unmoved as Jesus was crucified. They may very well have added a little ridicule of their own as the jeering mob hurled insults at him and made fun of him. They had no real opposition to him; they certainly felt no support for him. They were just there. If he died, so what? If he lived, so what? What difference did it make to them anyhow? If Jesus were dying on the cross in our time, that might well characterize the largest part of the crowd that would gather round the cross. That's the way many live, not taking anything very seriously.

There were also confused people there. They didn't altogether understand what was happening. They had had great hopes that

Jesus was the promised Messiah, the Deliverer who would come from God to break the yoke of the foreign oppressors who had ruled over Israel for too long. True, they really didn't understand who the Messiah was, or what he would do, but they had become pretty well convinced that Jesus just might be the one for whom they had been looking all along. But now, he who was supposed to deliver them from oppression was himself the victim of the cruelest kind of oppression. Instead of being a deliverer as they had hoped, he couldn't even help himself in this time of crisis. How was he to be of help to them? He had been speaking words of life to them, talking about overcoming sin and death. But now he was death's most prominent victim. And instead of being the victor over sin, he was apparently its helpless pawn, dying a death reserved only for sin's worst practitioners.

Confused people found their latent hopes shattered. Some of those who found their hopes shattered were his apostles. For them, the confusion and bitter disappointment must have been acute. After all, they had left everything they had in order to cast their lot with him. They had invested three years of their lives in following him, with the hope that he was about to usher in the kingdom of God. And they hoped that they might have authority in the coming kingdom. Indeed, two of them had even dared to ask to have the number one and number two places at Jesus' side. They didn't understand what they were asking, nor did they understand the kingdom that he was ushering in. But they had high hopes. And now their hopes were dying before their very eyes. What were they to do? What were they to think?

Even though Jesus had told them repeatedly that he would die—that it was necessary for him to die—not one of them understood why he was dying or what his death would accomplish. Even more to the point, he had also told them that he would be victorious over death—that he would be raised from the dead on the third day—not a one of them understood what he meant. The proof of that is in the realization that they were all surprised, even shocked, when they found the tomb empty and Jesus alive on the first Easter morning. To say that they were confused as they stood around the cross is to put it mildly. They didn't know what to make of the crucifixion of Jesus. They had had such high hopes for him, and now look! And what were they to do? The spirit of the angry mob that crucified him was such that they might turn on them also. Peter had already evidenced that fear when he denied three times that he even knew Jesus.

The world always has its confused people. They don't get the drift of things until it is too late. They chuckle at jokes after everyone else has long forgotten the punch line. They seek to capitalize on an opportunity after it has already passed them by. They make the wrong choices in life, more often than not, and live in regret afterward as they look back wishing they had taken the other fork of the road. Life always seems to be about two paces ahead of them and on the shelf above where they are. They seem to stumble through life, never too sure what to make of things about them.

But the confused men who stood about the cross were not that sort of folk. They were not like those who never seem to know what the score is. They were of a different lot. They were not easily taken in. They had been certain that they were right in following Jesus Christ, even at the expense of leaving their businesses, families, and so forth. But now, everything they believed in seemed to have come apart at the seams. If their Master could be so quickly rejected by the crowds, a victim of mob violence, what could they believe in? This was the confusion that tormented their minds.

There were others who might be described as seekers. They shared some of the feelings of those who were badly confused. They were people who had followed Jesus at some distance. They had not become closely involved with him. They were more casual in their relationship to him. They were sincere people who had felt the impact of his personal presence and had been stirred by his preaching and teaching.

What Jesus said seemed to carry authority—it had a ring of authenticity. As some others were to say after Jesus' resurrection, "Did not our hearts burn within us?" (Luke 24:32). They felt that something important was happening in Jesus. And they were looking to see if they ought to be involved. They were seeking something inexplicable to satisfy their inner longings and stirrings. When the rumor spread across town that Jesus was going to be executed that day, they were both repulsed and attracted by the awful scene. They had a strange, empty feeling when Jesus finally said, "Father, into thy hands I commit my spirit!" (Luke 23:46). Now it must have seemed to those who had been seeking that the search must go on, elsewhere. There are always those who are in a constant quest for something to give personal satisfaction and fulfillment. They go through life seeking, seldom finding real satisfaction.

There were others there that day who could best be described as deluded people. These were the people who thought they were doing God a favor by putting Jesus to death. They had recognized early in the ministry of Jesus that they were on a collision course with him. His religion was too radical. Indeed, his teaching would mean the end of religion as they knew it. His demands for a religion that should be demonstrated in daily life rather than in periodic ceremony was going a bit too far. And there was no compromise with him. He left them no choice. It was either his way or their way. Given those alternatives, it soon became clear to them that God was in danger as long as this man was around; or at least the comfortable religion they had identified with God was in danger of being overthrown by Jesus.

To these people there was only one thing to do. That was to do away with Jesus. It was not long after Jesus began his public ministry that certain men began plotting how they might discredit Jesus in the eyes of the popular masses. If they could trip him up with tricky questions, he might lose face with the crowds. But somehow their tricky questions always seemed to explode in their faces when he answered. And their criticisms of him always boomeranged and came whistling back at them with lightning speed. There was no way that they could simply trap him or embarrass him. Sterner measures were necessary.

They thought that God would smile approvingly if they could arrange for Jesus to be put to death. Indeed, they plotted to have him executed. It took some skulduggery to pull it off. They simply engineered his quiet betrayal by one of his own followers in an inconspicuous place and a rapid succession of six trials to give his death some air of respectability. When the crucial verdict of Pontius Pilate, the resident Roman governor, was about to go the wrong way, they managed to whip up enough public demonstration that Pilate was forced to wash his hands of the matter and let the angry mob have its way. It really doesn't take much ability to whip up mob sentiment, and this was a powerful tool in their plot to destroy Jesus. Not even Pilate felt that he was a match for an angry mob shouting, "Crucify him! Crucify him!" Pilate very well knew that if he didn't let them have their way he might become their victim instead.

These deluded men who thought that they were doing God a favor by killing Jesus got their way. And there they stood around the cross smirking and smiling, congratulating each other on a job well-done. Down inside they felt confident that God himself must be well pleased with them for the unusual service that they had rendered. How deluded people can be! This must have been the height of delusion.

There are some of these deluded people in every age. I once met a man who was a typical example. Years before, he had become critical of his pastor who was not running the church to suit him. He had started a movement to oust the pastor. After awhile he was successful. Only later did he realize how wrong he had been. It later came to light that the pastor was not guilty of the wrongs he had been charged with, and the congregation realized that he had been giving them better leadership than they realized. Moreover, the church had been almost irreparably harmed by the internal feud generated by firing the pastor. It was many years later when the shock waves finally subsided. The name of the church in the community had been badly harmed. The church found it extremely difficult to attract new members because of its notorious past in that small town. The man who had been instrumental in ousting the former pastor had lived in personal misery with a guilty conscience for some twenty years. He had thought he was doing right, but later realized that he had been badly deluded. And there were plenty like him around the cross.

There was another in the picture. For him life came into focus at the cross. He realized for the first time what it was all about. He too was dying, but by his own admission he was dying justly, for crimes that he had committed. As another criminal, also being executed, mocked Jesus, the first criminal spoke out in his defense. Somehow, he recognized Jesus for who he was. He also recognized himself as he really was. And the comparison was not good. Perhaps the best thing that he ever did was the heartfelt cry that came from his lips that day. "Remember me, Jesus, when you come as King!" (Luke 23:42, TEV). He had gotten the clearest perspective on life that he had ever had.

He wasn't the only one to find that life comes into focus at the cross. Across the centuries of time there have been countless others who have found themselves, and what the true meaning of life is, at the foot of the cross. What happened at the cross has made a profound difference in their lives. In many instances the cross has meant that shattered lives could be mended. It has meant that misdirected lives could be set on the right course. The cross has meant that listless lives could be made vital. The death of Jesus has provided a reason for living.

For those who have found that the cross makes a profound difference, the cross has become the marching banner of their lives. It has come to symbolize the deepest commitment of their hearts. With just a little imagination you can see a multitude of people who have marched under the banner of the cross and have left the world a far different place.

These who have marched under the banner of the cross are illustrated by a brilliant young man who was working in a rather good job in industry. He had a large income, with considerable opportunity for advancement with his company. But then he was converted. And he took his conversion seriously. His way of life became different; his values, his way of life, underwent quite a change. He became thoroughly involved in the work of his church. He began to share his Christian testimony with others, both at work and in his neighborhood. Still, he wasn't altogether satisfied. He felt that his life ought to mean something more than supervising production in an industrial plant. He wanted to make more of a contribution to the world than that. He wanted to be more of a Christian influence than he could through his present job.

He learned of an opportunity to teach in a Christian mission school. It seemed to him that he had the necessary qualifications, so he applied for the job, believing that God was leading him to invest his life in this specialized Christian ministry. Some of his friends and business associates were shocked when they learned that he was giving up a lucrative career with his company in order to take a teaching job paying only a fraction of what he was earning. But the impact of what Jesus had done for him on the cross had so moved him that he had to offer his life as a sacrifice for Jesus in return. He had taken the cross as the marching banner of his life.

The philosophy of the Christian who stands beneath the cross is well expressed by the words of John the Baptist. John was asked about Jesus and about his relationship to Jesus. John pointed out that it was his function in life to point to Jesus, not to himself. "This is how my own happiness is made complete. He must become more important while I become less important" (John 3:29-30, TEV). This must be the sentiment of one who has seen the cross for what it is. This ought to reflect the commitment of anyone who has understood what Jesus Christ has done for him.

This kind of commitment to Jesus Christ is shown beautifully in the life of a well-known businessman who for many years made a promise to God that he would try to speak to at least one person each day about becoming a Christian. And for many years he did exactly that. He took his own salvation seriously. He had seen the very shadow of the cross fall across him. The cross was the marching banner of his life. It symbolized what he was living for.

There were many kinds of people who stood about the cross when Jesus died. They had many kinds of reactions to what happened there. It would not be any different today if Jesus were crucified in a prominent spot in your town. There would be the same sprinkling of curious persons. There would still be some hardened who couldn't care less. There would still be some indifferent, really oblivious to what was going on. There would be some confused people who were bewildered by it all. There would still be some earnestly seeking a fuller life.

Yes, there would still be some who see life come into focus because of the cross. And they would make the cross the marching banner of their lives.

Where in that sea of faces about the cross are you? Which group characterizes you? That is the crucial question.

3
The Cross for the World

The modern news media has made a global village out of our world. Good and bad news alike is almost instantaneously flashed to the remotest corners of the earth. What is whispered in one corner of the earth is common knowledge for all the world only hours later. Who did not see the assassination of John F. Kennedy in Dallas, or the first steps of a man on the moon only a few years later? Who did not see the amazing feats of Olga Korbut, or the even more amazing performance of Nadia Komanici? Who did not sicken (or gloat!) a little more each day as the dirty linen of Watergate was publicly laundered for many months? Newspapers, radio, and television have reduced our world to a global village where both the important news items and a mass of trivia are poured out on us all day.

What a pity Jesus was not born and crucified in the twentieth century instead of the first! The whole world at once could have seen the babe in the manger. The whole world at once could have seen the cross—or the empty tomb that followed three days later. Instead, there is much of the world today that still does not know that there ever was a Jesus Christ, the Son of God, or that he died on a cross, or that he was raised from the dead on the third day. Still, if Jesus had been born in our day, he might have become instant news in a TV spectacular, and then almost as quickly forgotten. The modern news media, fine as it is at times, really would have been inadequate to interpret and report the world's greatest happening, the redemptive work of the Son of God who lived and died among us.

God knew best in sending his Son in an age that was less technologically advanced, when the spread of news was handled differently. After all it would take a special kind of reporting, witnessing out of a Spirit-charged heart, to adequately tell of the message of the cross. By today's standards, Jesus died on the cross in a remote time and an obscure place. Only a tiny percentage of the world's people alive at that time ever heard of Jesus or his cross.

But the cross was by no means an event meant to be limited to the first century, or even to ancient Palestine. In the mind of God the cross was meant to be the central event in all of history, with a vital significance for all men, of all times, of all places. The tragedy is that much of the world today still does not know of the cross, or at least does not really understand the significance of the cross.

Consider the meaning of that cross for the whole world. First of all, it must be understood as a burden that existed in the heart of God long before there was ever a cross standing on Calvary. There was already a cross in God's heart before a shouting mob took Jesus outside Jerusalem to see him crucified. In fact, there never would have been a cross on Golgotha with the Son of God dying upon it if there had not already been a cross in the heart of God.

The heart of God had long ached over the lost condition of humanity. As God looked out on the world he had created, he saw that sin had entered his creation. He saw that human beings had rebelled against their Maker and were held as prisoners of sin. Sin was like an alien force holding humanity prisoner, inflicting torture, and perverting lives. To say that God was distressed by the fallen condition of humanity would be the understatement. He saw that each human was helpless and in despair. Humanity could do nothing to become free from the entangling web of sin. None could conquer the alien force at work within. People could not produce the righteousness expected of them by a holy God. Perhaps it is a toss-up whether humanity's greatest problem is an inner rebelliousness or the alien power of evil which confronts each person on every side. In either case, humanity's need is the same: help must come from beyond each individual if a person is to be saved out of his helplessness and hopelessness.

From the beginning it is evident that God cares for humanity, and that God *loves* all people in spite of their sin. There is a heart of love within God that will not let him rest while human beings need help. As we look back across God's dealings with humanity, we see clearly that God has long been at work showing his love to people, both in word and in action. And that love is a costly love. For God was moving, inexorably, a step at a time, in terms of the ancient sacrificial system, toward that day when he would offer his incarnate Son as a sacrificial Lamb upon the altar of the cross as the ultimate sacrifice, assuring the forgiveness of all sin. Thus there was already a cross in God's heart—an intense burden leading to the ultimate act of sacrifice—before there was ever a cross on Calvary.

But the cross was more than a burden in God's heart. It was an action: a stark, crude, cruel, rugged cross on Calvary with the Son of God hanging on it in horrible, shameful death. The cross in the Christian message is not just a philosophy, not just a principle or an influence set forth in the world. It was a dramatic action on the part of God. The cross may have been erected by sinful people in the worst act of rebellion against the Creator ever perpetrated. But it was within the will of God. When properly understood, God was in full control. The cross was the price God had to pay to do what had to be done to free people from sin and provide eternal salvation.

In a world where sin was taken lightly, there had to be a dramatic action on the part of God to break the hold of sin upon man. The cross was the action of God in bringing divine judgment upon sin; the cross was the supreme judgment of God upon sin. The cross shows to the world in the most dramatic way possible what sin deserves as God sees it. Let no person henceforth think lightly of his or her misdeeds, whatever their nature. In God's eyes any deviation from the standard of righteousness set by God himself is infinitely serious and stands judged and condemned in the cross.

The cross was an action of God redeeming humanity. The cross was the price God had to pay to reclaim persons for himself. This was no bookkeeping transaction of so much suffering in order to bring about so much redemption. This was what it cost God to step into the human situation and claim humanity as rightfully his when humanity was in the very act of rebellion. The very persons God came to save crucified the Son of God who came to tell of God's forgiving love.

Perhaps the cross as an action of redemption is illustrated best by the example of Hosea. Hosea was an Old Testament prophet who found that his beloved wife, Gomer, had become unfaithful to him. In fact, he found that she had become a common prostitute and now was being offered for sale as a slave. God told Hosea to go to the marketplace and purchase (*redeem*) his fallen wife, take her home, lavish his love upon her, and restore her to his bosom as his beloved wife once more. In one sense, the price Hosea paid was small: one could buy a worn-out prostitute pretty cheaply. In another sense, Hosea paid a great price: he had already had to endure intense heartbreak as his love was spurned; now he was having to endure the shame of going into the public marketplace to buy back the one who had spurned his love. And even as he was doing this Gomer was probably wondering what that fool Hosea was doing in bidding to buy her. It was only after Hosea had had time to lavish his love upon Gomer once more that she came to understand what he was doing.

It was in this way that God paid a great price to redeem humanity from sin. He entered the human situation through the incarnation of his Son who endured humiliation and the shame heaped upon him by those he came to save, and finally died as the Lamb of God slain from the foundation of the world. The cross was thus an action of redemption on the part of God as he stooped to save us from our sin.

The cross was also an action of proclamation. Through the cross God was proclaiming the message of his forgiveness, his offer of salvation, and new life in Christ to all men. Today wherever the cross is heralded in song or sermon, wherever it is placed on a necklace or a steeple, it is intended as a silent but vivid reminder of God's costly offer of salvation to lost men. The cross was God expressing his love for lost mankind in the most dramatic way open to him. When men today realize what the cross really means, they are awestruck by the depth and intensity of the love that God has for them. It is utterly unthinkable that God's Son would die on a cross in order to save men who were in rebellion against God, and yet that is precisely what has happened. The cross was, then, God's action in proclaiming his infinite love for man.

The cross signifies God's intention of changing sinful men and their society. God intensely desires to save all men. In fact, he is doing all that he can, consistent with the freedom of the will that he has given man, to bring men to salvation. He is still at work in his world trying to work out his purposes in human society. He is trying to bring about a civilization which honors justice and righteousness and love and other such worthy Christian values.

The only real hope humanity has for changing society is through the message of the cross, the redeeming grace of God. Social reform and sociological engineering have their place in human society, but the greatest hope we have for working a substantial change in our society is the message of the cross: we can be made anew through Jesus Christ. Christian people ought to attack the problems of sin and suffering in every conceivable way open to them, but let them never forget that the ultimate answer to all of the ills of the world is the message of the cross. The cross was God's way of offering new life to the world. *The cross for the world.*

But much of the world goes on its way, unaware of the cross. For them it is as though Jesus had never come at all. *The world without a cross.* How ironic that Jesus died for all people, of all times, of all places, yet, two thousand years later many still do not know of that cross. Many more may be vaguely aware that the cross is somehow the symbol identified with Christianity, but they really have no idea what the cross means.

The world without the cross is a world in darkness. It is a world in the worst kind of darkness: spiritual darkness. It is a world where sin is still rampant even though God is trying to point us to the ultimate remedy for sin. Even in our own land, sometimes called a Christian nation, it is not safe to walk alone on the streets of some of our major cities even in daytime, let alone at night. The newspapers daily reflect man's inhumanity to his fellowman. Morality is in shambles. Gross immorality and shameful perversion make a mockery of any reasonable pretense of righteousness. In many ways modern society has not advanced very far from the primitive ways of the jungle.

In this world of spiritual darkness there are many who have never heard the good news of the gospel of Jesus Christ. There are more lost people alive in the world today than have lived in all of the centuries combined since the time that Jesus himself lived upon the earth. That fact ought to stagger the mind of the sensitive Christian when it is considered. In a day of instant global communications there are still so many people who have not yet heard of the message of the cross and of the new life in Christ that is available to them. A world without a cross!

Some might think that I am talking only about remote islands of the Pacific Ocean, or the interior villages of China, or remote tribes in Africa. But many of these who have never heard of Jesus Christ are our next-door neighbors here in our own homeland. They live within the shadow of our churches and still do not know what the gospel offers to them. Consider one example which probably represents many people in our land.

Years ago I was pastor of the First Southern Baptist Church in Chula Vista, California, a lovely suburb of San Diego. One day a pretty young woman came to my study to keep an appointment that she had made a day or two earlier by telephone. She was engaged to be married to a young Navy man who was a Baptist. The Navy chaplain who was going to marry them in a few weeks had suggested to her that she should talk to a clergyman of her fiance's faith as part of her preparation for marriage. She had come to me wanting to know who Baptists are and what they stand for. I quickly discovered that she knew nothing about Christianity in general, much less Baptists in particular.

As we talked about the meaning of Christianity and faith in Jesus Christ as Savior I read John 3:16 to her. I had it underlined in that particular Bible so that I could easily hand it to someone to read. When I reached across the desk and placed my Bible in her hands, she grew as white as a sheet. Her hands began to tremble.

I asked, "What's the matter?"

She replied with a shaky voice, "That's the first time I ever saw a Bible."

Yet she had been born and reared not more than six blocks from a gospel-preaching church, in a city of many Evangelical churches. Still she had never seen a Bible or heard the Christian gospel of the cross. And that in a land where the Bible has been the number 1 best-seller on book lists for more years than anyone remembers. That was not in some isolated spot of heathenism in a remote part of the earth. That was on Main Street, U.S.A., where

Bibles can be bought with pocket change at drugstores and variety stores in any city, where virtually all our cities are dotted with gospel-preaching churches. A world without a cross!

The world without a cross is a world groping, staggering along trying to find its way. It is a world living under the constant threat of a nuclear holocaust in the ultimate war. It is a world divided East against West, black against white, rich against poor, young against old. Great problems seemingly defy solutions. The world seems to stagger from one crisis to another. We fought World War I to end all wars. We again fought to end all wars in World War II. And there has scarcely been a day of peace since the armistice was signed to end World War II. There was Korea, Vietnam, the various Middle East conflicts, the Irish civil war with two so-called Christian factions fighting each other. The whole world seems like a powder keg with an already smoldering fuse.

It is not only a world in the collective sense that is groping, trying to find its way in spiritual darkness. The same figure characterizes so many of the world's people individually. There are so many people today who are frustrated with empty, meaningless lives. They have a gnawing, spiritual hunger. No, they do not realize that their acute problem is a spiritual emptiness. But they are acutely aware that something is wrong, that there must be something more to life than they have found. They buy millions of books on how to forget their troubles and find fulfillment in life. They spend billions of dollars on entertainment and gadgets to distract them from the awesome emptiness that is in their hearts. Many of them are lured into a weird assortment of cults as they grope about, trying to find a sense of direction in life. They wander about like mice in a maze trying to find their way through to some token reward at the other end.

I had an experience years ago that illustrates the lost, groping feeling that many people have throughout their lifetimes. I lived in an old house that did not have light switches on the wall to turn on the ceiling light. Instead, each light had a pull chain that hung beneath it. One night the telephone rang about 2:00 AM. I roused from a deep sleep and started trying to find the light chain. I was standing in a very dark bedroom, swinging crazily around in the air, trying to find the light chain. I finally gave up on the light chain, thinking that it might be easier to find the telephone in the other end of the house. I stumbled around in the dark, falling over furniture as I went. When I finally got to the telephone, I picked up the receiver just in time to hear the line go dead with a *click* as the calling party hung up. I was so sleepy when I first awoke that I was disoriented in the darkened room. And the house was so dark that night that I simply could not see even when I was fully awake. I was stumbling all around.

Many people seem to spend a lifetime like that, not quite sure where they are, stumbling about as they try to find their way through life. And they are filled with a spiritual longing that they do not quite understand. I once heard a missionary tell of a brief trip that he made into an East European country where he had some limited opportunities to preach. One day on a street corner a stranger came up to him with a carefully wrapped package in his hand. He proceeded to open it, taking from a little box a single printed sheet that was obviously very old and tattered. Through the evangelist's interpreter, he inquired if his yellowed sheet were a page from the Bible. As the interpreter and the evangelist examined it they saw that it was a page out of the book of Exodus. It was all of the Bible that the old man had ever seen. When he was told that indeed it was a page from the Bible, he carefully wrapped it up again and clutched it to his breast. As he disappeared back into the crowd they wondered if he really understood the end of the story towards which Exodus points: the cross of Jesus Christ and the deliverance from sin available through Jesus Christ.

The world without a cross! Though Jesus came and died to bring men salvation nearly two thousand years ago, there are still so very, very many people who are without the message of the cross. They are crying out for help as they grope their way through life—and they are not finding it. A missionary to Japan tells of his next-door neighbors whom he had tried to lead to Christ. But they were ardent devotees of one of the Eastern religions. However, the missionary said, one day he saw a big bonfire in his neighbor's yard. He went out to see what the occasion was. To his surprise he found that his neighbors were burning their family's idol.

He asked why they were burning their god in a bonfire. The husband exclaimed, "We've prayed to our god again and again, but he never hears us!" They were heartsick with a god who wouldn't answer, indeed, who could not answer. They were typical of that world without a cross, groping about in spiritual darkness, living with hungry hearts. There are many, many people leaning on false hopes, depending on gods which cannot answer. Only Jesus Christ can make good on the promise, "Come to me, all who labor and are heavy laden, and I will give you rest" (Matt. 11:28). There are still many who are burdened with spiritual ignorance, primitive superstitions, and crushing personal burdens. Help has come through Jesus Christ, but they are still ignorant of his birth, still ignorant of his death, still ignorant of his triumphant resurrection and ascension. They do not know that they could now have him in their hearts as an ever-present companion, guide, and source of strength. They are part of a world still without a cross.

The world without a cross is a world in inky darkness, groping about in heart-hunger, following mirages. A mirage is a tantalizing vision of a beautiful oasis in the distance on a hot, barren desert. It can look very real and inviting, but you can never get there. It always recedes before your eyes, vanishing when you most urgently want to reach it. It is an optical illusion that often plays tricks on weary travelers.

I remember the first time I saw a mirage. It was a blistering hot day and we were weary with travel in the hot sun. Off in the desert we saw what looked like a lake with a grove of beautiful shade trees. We were all set for a swim and then a nap under the trees; only, after an hour or more of travel, we found that the inviting vision had disappeared.

Some of the world without a cross is following mirages of various descriptions. These mirages are panaceas offered for the cure of man's pressing problems. Communism, for instance, has enjoyed steady growth, especially in the underdeveloped countries of the world. It has had a powerful appeal to people who have had little other basis for hope. But it has been able to deliver only a tiny fraction of what it has promised in the visions that it holds forth to attract converts. More than a new economic system is needed to supply man's deepest needs. Nationalism is another of the mirages with a powerful appeal to some of the people who have long been held in unfortunate circumstances. But those who have achieved political independence are finding that it will take more than a new political framework to solve man's greatest problems.

Many have followed the mirage of education as a panacea for people's ills. While education has contributed greatly to humanity's progress, education cannot supply the new inner person which is needed if humanity is to make strides forward. Others have depended on the mirage of social welfare programs and sociological engineering to try to meet the pressing needs of man. But sociology, even though it has contributed greatly to solving some of man's problems, cannot deliver all that it promises. It, too, cannot touch the soul of a man. Only the gospel of the One who died on the cross can provide a new man. Only Jesus Christ, who died on a cross for the world, can make men new. Only he who made men in the first place can make men anew.

Man's deepest problem, the problem which is at the base of all of his other problems, is the problem of a sinful soul in rebellion against God. Only the message of the new life that comes through Jesus Christ can change the soul of a man and make him anew. That is the message of the cross, but much of the world goes on its way without a cross.

Ironically, the answer is already here. God gave himself to the world through the cross in the early part of the first century. Jesus commanded his followers to take the message of the cross victory over sin and death to all the world. Now, almost two thousand years later much of the world is still waiting for the message to arrive. It is a world hurting as it waits, a world groping in darkness as it waits. It waits, not really understanding that it is waiting, lost in its delusion and sin.

A story by a Christian layman made a vivid impression on me as he told about the world waiting for the good news of the gospel of Jesus Christ. This layman was an oil field worker. He had been part of a pipeline crew working in one of the Middle Eastern countries. Frequently his crew camped on the desert as they followed the pipeline route, checking on equipment and valves, and so forth. Several of the men on this pipeline crew were Christians. At night when they were camped on the desert they held evangelistic services, sharing the gospel with nomadic desert tribesmen, or nearby villagers.

One night as one of the laymen was preaching he noticed that a tall, stately-looking man had crept up to the outer edge of the circle. When the service was over and the group of people were leaving, the stately-looking man came to the layman who had preached and asked, "How long have you known this Jesus you preached about?"

The layman answered, "I have known Jesus most of my life."

The Arab chieftain asked again, "And did your father know him, too?"

"Why, yes, my father knew him also."

"And what about your father's father?"

"My grandfather also knew Jesus. In fact all of my family, as far back as we can trace our history, have been Christians."

The Arab prince thought for a moment, drew a deep breath, and shouted in a booming voice, "If you, and your father, and your father's father, have known about Jesus all of this time, *why in the world are you just now telling us?*"

That's the question that a world waiting in darkness must ask of those of us who have the light of the world in Jesus Christ. "Why in the world are you just now telling us?" The cross happened nearly two thousand years ago, but there is still a world without a cross, ignorant of the salvation that has come through Jesus Christ. Still ignorant of the new life that is available. Still waiting for us to bring the message of the good news that God offers us his life-changing grace.

The hope of a world that is stumbling about in spiritual ignorance and darkness is the message of the cross. The cross is the key to unlock men's hearts. It is the key to unlock the shackles of sin that bind them in misery and godlessness. The cross is the key to unlock the door to a bright future for a world where the future now looks pretty dim, at best.

The cross is meant to be a hope for all persons, not just a chosen few. God intended the message of the cross for all people of all times. The pity is that so many are still waiting for the good news that God cares enough to offer a revolutionary power to transform sinful lives and change wicked societies. Unfortunately, many have never heard of the cross, and many more who have seen the symbol of the cross all of their lives only know that it is some sort of religious symbol without really knowing what it means. It was God's intention for the cross to serve as an announcement to the world that his redeeming grace is open to all, as Paul put it, "For, every one who calls upon the name of the Lord will be saved" (Rom. 10:13), quoting an ancient prophet, Joel.

Proclaiming the cross is the number 1 business of God's people. Indeed, proclaiming the message of the victory of Jesus over sin and death is at the heart of all our Christian responsibility. All else that we do as Christians hinges upon this central responsibility. It is a responsibility which comes to us in many dimensions. One dimension is that of individual witnessing to the saving power of Jesus Christ wherever our life circumstances might take us. In effect, you may have the responsibility of being a missionary to the oil field where you work on a drilling rig, or a missionary in the large office complex where you work. You have the responsibility of being a missionary on the school grounds where you are a student, or in the grocery store where you shop. Each of us has opportunities, perhaps daily, to bear witness through word and deed to the saving grace of God.

Another dimension of the responsibility of proclaiming the cross is in the need for missionaries who go from their natural home environment to live and minister in another culture, sharing the gospel with all they can. God today calls out missionaries just as surely as he called Paul and Barnabas to be the first missionaries. What the world needs today, if the message of the cross is to reach the uttermost parts of the earth, is people with the commitment of William L. (Bill) Wallace who chose to stay on duty as a missionary doctor instead of fleeing to safety when extreme danger from Communism threatened. What is needed is men with the commitment of J. Lewis Shuck who responded to a plea for a missions offering with a scrap of paper on which he had written, "Having nothing else to give, I give myself." He became one of Southern Baptists' pioneer missionaries to China. What is needed is the commitment of Mrs. William J. David, a pioneer missionary to

Africa. She had already given several of her children to death in the terrible toll that tropical diseases once took on the American white man. When she lay dying, her last words to her husband were, "Never, never give up Africa."

The cross must become a commanding vision to God's people. We must see the world without a cross and understand its anguish as it gropes in spiritual ignorance. We must see the cross for the world as God saw it, the hope for all mankind. As the people of God, we must have the compassion and conviction to take the cross as our marching banner to the waiting world.

4
The Center of History

The cross of Jesus Christ is the center point of all history. To the eye of faith, everything that happened before the cross was a preparation for that pivotal moment. Everything that has happened since the cross is part of God's grand design of working out his purpose in history by means of the cross. The cross towers over all of time.

Not all understand the cruciality of the cross. Not all realize its strategic significance in the overall scheme of things. But when the tapestry of world history is finally concluded, it will be seen clearly that the cross was the central event in the whole span of time. It will be seen as the master key that supplies the meaning of human history as a whole. The cross is like a giant axle on which the world has been spinning from the beginning. True, the cross was not seen by persons from the beginning, but the cross was firmly fixed in God's mind from the very first. The cross was revealed to humanity only when the time was right. Even now, the cross is still unknown to vast multitudes of people, and millions more do not understand its central significance in what is happening in the onward march of world history.

But when time is ended and the new order of eternity has been fully ushered in, all shall see the central place of the cross in what God has been doing from the beginning. The cross—and by that symbol I mean the whole startling event of the birth, life, death, and resurrection of Jesus—stands at the very center of our understanding of history. Indeed, the whole Western world expresses that very thought each time the date is written. Our calendar itself bears witness that Jesus Christ stands at the center of history. For whether we are talking about the death of Julius Caesar on March 15, 44 BC, or the birth of George Washington on AD February 22, 1732, we are affirming the centrality of Jesus Christ in human history. Some may not know it, but BC stands for *before Christ* and AD stands for *anno Domini,* or *in the year of the Lord.* For many centuries now, our way of reckoning time in the Western world has been done by relating events to the central event of Jesus Christ. We say that historical events happened so many years before or after Jesus Christ.

The cross, the central event in the life of Jesus Christ, stands at the center of attention in the tapestry of time. From the Christian point of view, all we know of the work of God prior to the time of Jesus was a preparation for the great revelation of God's saving love in the cross of God's Son. The cross was not an isolated event that God suddenly thrust upon an unsuspecting world without any advance preparation. There is a clear line of preparation for the cross that reaches back over many hundreds of years as God prepared, a step at a time, for the central event of all time: that day when his loving concern for dying men would be fully and dramatically revealed. "But when the time had fully come, God sent forth his Son, born of woman, born under the law, to redeem those who were under the law, so that we might receive adoption as sons" (Gal. 4:4-5).

When the time had fully come! God had been preparing for the central event of history for a long time. Indeed, if you want to understand why Jesus came into our world and died on the cross as the central event of all time, you need to go back to the dawning of human history; all the way back to the Garden of Eden; all the way back to the creation and humanity's first steps upon the earth.

In the beautiful setting of the Garden of Eden, where God had provided bountifully for all of Adam and Eve's needs and enjoyed an intimacy of fellowship with them that we can scarcely understand, the unthinkable happened. They rebelled against their Creator in a deliberate act of self-will in rejecting the clear command of their Creator. In retrospect, we are shocked that such a thing could have happened. Yet, at the same time, each of us comes to realize that we have done the same thing. We, too, have violated the clear command of God. And, as with Adam and Eve, we may not have realized what we were doing at the moment; certainly we did not realize the serious consequences of it. We may excuse ourselves somewhat by rationalizing that we live in a sinful world which has been corrupted by all of the sins that have resulted across the centuries from the sin of the first two people on the earth. But that is too simple and self-serving. We cannot excuse ourselves that easily.

As we look back at Adam and Eve in a setting of innocence, living in an ideal setting untouched by any kind of sin and corruption, their sin is shocking to us. But it was no surprise to God. In his infinite wisdom, God already knew that humanity would sin against him. And God already knew what he would do when that happened. He was not caught unawares with the shock of humanity's sin. He was not left wondering what to do, having to take some unforeseen, alternative action.

God already knew that he would respond both with judgment and forgiveness. For it is his innermost nature to deal decisively with sin and redemptively with the sinner. As we look back from our vantage point of several thousand years of the history of God's redeeming activity, we can see that there was a cross in the heart of God from the beginning and that it was inevitable that the cross should become firmly rooted at the very center of history. It is no wonder that Paul could say, "When the time had fully come!" What had been implicit from the beginning was brought into shocking reality at the most strategic moment of history. God put his only Son on the cross in the ultimate act of redemption, judging sin before all the world and laying bare his gracious, redeeming love for all people.

The world was not ready for the cross, however, when Adam and Eve took the fatal step into sin. Many steps lay between the Garden of Eden and the hill of Calvary. Man was not ready for the dramatic action of the cross. He could not have comprehended its crucial importance if it had come at the beginning of history. The depth of its meaning would have escaped him entirely. Even now we are staggered at the significance of the cross of Jesus Christ. Our minds grope for an adequate understanding of how the cross of Jesus Christ becomes the instrument by which God brings forgiveness and reconciliation to us.

That the cross is crucial to our salvation is perfectly clear to the eye of faith. *How* the cross becomes the instrument of God's redemptive activity on our behalf goes so far beyond our little understanding that we can only bow in reverence before the cross. The very fact of the number and variety of interpretations of how the cross saves bears witness to the profound depths of the significance of what God did through the death of Jesus Christ.

What happened in the Garden of Eden? What did God do in response? Both of these questions need to be answered if we are to understand the cross that stands at the focal point of history. The action of Adam and Eve constituted an open act of defiance against God, and it brought on them the consequences that they had been warned about from the beginning. While it is true that they acted in response to the prompting of the tempter, the fact remains that they acted fully on their own and were totally responsible for their sin. Their sin brought serious consequences not only upon themselves but upon their posterity. In a sense their sin set up a chain reaction of sinning that goes on until this very day. The world's first murder came in the immediate family of Adam and Eve. But all of us who have sinned in our own time can no more pass the blame for our sin back to Adam than Adam could pass the blame either to Eve or to Satan. Adam made his rebellious choice in sin and we are fully responsible for our choice in sinning.

It is pointless for us to speculate what might have happened if Adam had not sinned, for Adam did sin. And so has every other human being. The sobering words uttered in condemnation of the Israelites at a particular time during the period of the judges pretty accurately characterizes every age: "Every man did what was right in his own eyes" (Judg. 17:6). But God knew that it would be this way from the very beginning. God knew that in giving humans a free will they would misuse their freedom and neglect their responsibility. But when God created people, he wanted free, rational creatures who could respond to God's approach and enter into personal relationship with him. He did not want a mechanical robot, programmed to do and say all the right things at the push of a button. So, God created people in innocence and freedom, fully aware that he would have to deal with their sin and rebellion and all that those awful ideas imply.

God knew that people would sin and need to be forgiven. God knew that people would rebel and would need to be reconciled.

God knew that people would be corrupted and would need to be regenerated. God knew that people would fall and need to be lifted up; he also knew that people would be enslaved and would need to be redeemed. God knew that people would die spiritually and would need to be born again. He knew that people would be lost and would need to be saved; he also knew that people would be condemned and would need to be justified. God knew all of this and more about humanity's pitiful plight. And God was not unprepared to meet any of these needs. When God created man from the dust of the ground and breathed the breath of life into his nostrils, this was only the beginning of God's work in creating the humanity that he ultimately desired. For God knew that even this first man would turn away into sin and that then many things would have to be done across a vast period of time until God could accomplish his ultimate purpose in humanity.

The tragedy in Eden was no surprise to God and he was not caught unprepared. He immediately went into action, moving toward the distant central point of history, the cross of Jesus Christ. The first step in that direction was to come in the cool of the evening, looking for Adam as he usually did. Only this time Adam and Eve were hiding in the shame of their sin. When he found them, he pronounced the promised judgment upon them, sending them out of the ease of life in Eden into a world where they would not only endure the punishment for their sin, but would begin to learn the difficult lessons of obedience, responsibility, and faith since they would be tutored by God in both adversity and triumph. Notice that God did not put upon them more than they could bear or leave them without hope. He provided for their immediate needs in giving them clothing to cover their nakedness in their shamed condition. He did not put them to instant death as well he might have. But most important, notice that he did not leave them without hope.

God uttered a word of hope to Adam and Eve. It was a veiled word of hope that they could not have fully understood at that point. But it was a word of hope, which we can now see more clearly, as we look backwards, pointed toward the center point of history. God said in a word of judgment spoken to the tempter,

"I will put enmity between you and the woman,

and between your seed and her seed;

he shall bruise your head,

and you shall bruise his heel" (Gen. 3:15).

It is a mistake to read the full New Testament doctrine of salvation into this one veiled verse, but it is a promise of hope to the first pair who had just fallen in sin. It is God's first step toward the cross at the center of history. But it is only a first step and there are many more steps before God can provide the climactic moment of the full revelation of his redemption through Jesus Christ.

When Adam and Eve were cast out of the Garden of Eden, they were at square 1 on the long trail to where God was leading humanity, the perfection of unhindered spiritual unity with God. Adam and Eve were created in the image of God, with a definite godlikeness and in an unhindered relationship to him. But they were anything but that now. It was a long way to maturity in Christ, the goal that we shall later see as God's goal for people. But God moved Adam to square 1 on that long journey for human beings when he gave that first slight hint that they were not without hope.

One can follow the unfolding story of God's self-revelation throughout the Old Testament. Through successive stages, God was moving toward the cross and the supreme revelation of his redemptive righteousness and forgiving love through the death of Jesus Christ.

The first lesson that human beings had to learn was God's utter, complete opposition to sin. The account of God's judgment on sin through the flood of Noah's day could scarcely be a more dramatic and forceful lesson. Equally forceful is the lesson that the only people who survive the judgment of God are those who live with faith in God. Only the gracious provision of God for the few people of faith brought salvation for any.

The story of Noah is the sternest possible reminder for all time that the righteousness of God is utterly opposed to sin and only those who honor God in faithful obedience can expect to escape his judgment. God was teaching that there is no escape from judgment and that salvation comes only from God. A lost world could not understand the cross apart from the realization of God's unalterable opposition to sin. The lost must also understand that salvation comes only to those with genuine faith in God; otherwise the cross is useless. God was moving a step nearer to the cross in the dramatic events of Noah's day.

The lesson of faith is not easy to communicate, however. It cannot be written once and forgotten. Neither is it quickly comprehended in all its implications. Faith and obedience before God have dimensions that are still coming to light with the changing of times. So God took positive steps to create a people founded on faith who in turn might become a blessing to the world at large as the vehicle of knowledge about God. If people were ever to be ready for the central point of history, the life, death, and resurrection of God's Son, Jesus Christ, God would have to build a broad platform of revelation, making more and more of himself known so that they would be ready for the final stage of revelation through the cross of Jesus Christ.

No first grader in school learns to read by plunging into Shakespeare or Camus. No beginner in school starts learning mathematics at the level of calculus. A lot of groundwork must be laid before that little child is ready for these advanced academic disciplines. So it was with the human race. People could not suddenly be confronted with the full truth of the cross. God could only lead up to the cross a little at a time.

God reached into an obscure place, Ur of the Chaldees, and called Abram, whose name meant exalted father, to leave his home and follow him in faith to a land that he then did not even know. God's promise to Abram was that he would make of him a mighty nation, one that would be a source of blessing to all the world. Abram responded in positive faith and God took another step toward the cross. Abram's name was changed to Abraham, meaning father of a multitude, and God proceeded to develop his chosen people, chosen to be a blessing. Through Abraham and his descendants, God was creating a people of faith, a living demonstration to the world of the power of the God who stands above all. Abraham's grandson, Jacob, became the father of the twelve patriarchs of Israel, from whom descended the twelve tribes of Israel. Through this vast expanding family, God was creating a future nation through whom the world's Savior would come.

The children of Israel had to pass through the crucible of four hundred years of slavery in Egypt as part of the process of developing within them the peculiar consciousness of their calling. God had to raise up a Moses to be a deliverer to them. Not only did the Israelites find the deliverance of God through the instrumentality of Moses' leadership, but God used Moses to further regulate the practice of worship, teaching the people they must come to God on God's terms and not their own. Moses was also instrumental in teaching the people the moral requirements as well as the religious requirements of a holy God. And again God was moving nearer to the cross.

When Israel was finally established in the Promised Land as a nation in her own right, God raised up the prophets to denounce the sins of the people and reinforce the religious and moral expectations that God had for them. These same prophets repeatedly warned of impending judgment on those who took the requirements of God lightly. These same prophets also pointed forward to the time when God's Messiah would come. Again, God was moving toward the cross. Read through the eyes of faith, the history of the world up until the time of Jesus Christ was all a preparation for his coming and the full revelation of God's salvation being wrought through Jesus. Finally, Paul could say, "When the time had fully come!"

We cannot be fully sure of all that Paul was saying in that striking statement. Surely it includes all of the steps of preparation that God had made in the process of making himself known to his people. He may have been saying even more. The particular time in history was providential. Two or three hundred years earlier or later would have found considerably different circumstances. This particular time found the known civilized world in a period of stability and peace such as had hardly characterized the world in any other age. It was the best possible time for the church to get a start on the task of penetrating the whole world with the gospel of Jesus Christ. In addition to a strong stable government which united the whole Mediterranean world, there was a good system of roads and a common language, Greek, which made it most favorable for the spread of the gospel. Perhaps Paul was saying, "When God had carefully set the stage, he sent forth his Son." The time was right. The central moment of history had come. This was the moment to which God had been working since the beginning. No wonder that those who made our modern calendar set the time of Jesus as the dividing point of all of history—*before Christ* and *in the year of the Lord!*

When you stand at the cross, it is as though you are standing on top of Mount Everest and looking down on all the rest of the world. The cross is the continental divide of history to the eye of faith. All of history either flows to it or out from it.

Even the earthly life and teaching of Jesus seem directed towards the cross. From early in his ministry it was obvious that he was obsessed with a purpose that he must accomplish. It was not long until it was obvious that he was on a collision course with the religious establishment of his day. But neither family nor friends could turn him aside from his compelling purpose which would ultimately mean his death on the cross. When his disciples began to realize who he was, the Messiah-Son of God, he began from that point on in his life to teach concerning his coming death and resurrection. He saw his death and resurrection as his victory, the accomplishment of the very thing that he had come to do.

The cross, and the events immediately preceding it, are the most dramatic possible revelation of God's judgment on sin and his loving forgiveness. No author ever penned a more gripping drama of suspense and pathos than was acted out in real-life agony by Jesus. When the shadow of the cross was already falling across Jesus, he spent three unforgettable hours in the garden of Gethsemane praying his way through to the final commitment to the cross as the climactic step in accomplishing God's plan of salvation. Sin entered the world in the Garden of Eden. Jesus made the final commitment to the defeat of sin, even at the cost of his own death, in the garden of Gethsemane. And in another garden, where Jesus had lain in a tomb for three days, God sealed the doom of sin and death by raising his Son from the dead.

From that agonizing time in prayer, when weary disciples could not stay awake to pray with him, Jesus went rapidly through a succession of six illegal trials. Sentence was passed upon him by the default of the system of justice of his day. He was quickly led away amid the jeers and cheers of a riotous mob and he was crucified on a cross, perhaps the cruelest kind of execution known to man. But this was no defeat—neither for Jesus, nor for his heavenly Father. It was the moment of Jesus' victory. And it was the climax of God's long process of revealing his saving grace to sinful men. This was the moment that gave meaning to all that God had been doing from the creation of the world until this very time. Everything prior to Calvary was, in a sense, preparation for the cross. Everything since Calvary is the application of the saving gospel to the world of sinful men.

Don't misunderstand the cross as a single, isolated event that took place in a six-hour period from the nailing of Jesus to the cross to the moment when he cried, "Father, into thy hands I commit my spirit" (Luke 23:46). When we speak of the cross in this context as the climactic point of history, we must include the whole life and teaching of Jesus which preceded the cross and the resurrection and ascension of Jesus which followed the cross. In a sense, these all form one event which must not be torn apart. It is in this sense that Jesus spoke from the cross, shortly before his death, "It is finished" (John 19:30). What God had been doing from the beginning had now been brought to a climax in his earthly life.

What happened on that cross has a crucial importance for all men. Though our little minds cannot explain all that happened on the cross, it is of strategic importance. Jesus himself said in reference to his crucifixion, "And I, when I am lifted up from the earth, will draw all men to myself" (John 12:32). There is a demanding finality about what God was doing through Jesus Christ. John said of Jesus, "For God so loved the world that he gave his only Son, that whoever believes in him should not perish but have eternal life. For God sent the Son into the world, not to condemn the world, but that the world might be saved through him. He who believes in him is not condemned; he who does not believe is condemned already, because he has not believed in the name of the only Son of God" (John 3:16-18). John summed up this forceful statement concerning the cruciality of Jesus and his cross by saying, "He who believes in the Son has eternal life; he who does not obey the Son shall not see life, but the wrath of God rests upon him" (v. 36).

Thus all of history looked forward to the time when this all-encompassing grace of God should be revealed in the salvation made available through the cross of Jesus Christ. And all of history from a religious perspective now looks back to that crucial moment when God acted decisively to make the most profound revelation that he loves with a redeeming and forgiving love.

The cross stands at the center of history. All that has followed since the cross is the story of God's attempts through the church to get the message of new life in Christ to the people who are yet perishing in the agony of their sins. It is a marvelous story to trace the spread of the gospel out from the cross to millions of people scattered all over the world. In all the centuries since the cross God has been calling out a people for himself, giving them the responsibility of proclaiming the gospel of Jesus Christ. At the same time, there is a sad note to it all. For the spread has been painfully slow in some ages and in some places. There are still so many who have not heard the gospel. But God is moving from the cross toward his ultimate goal in history through the preaching of the cross.

Not only is the cross the center of history, with the modern Western world measuring history by what led up to the cross and what followed the time of Jesus, but the cross is also the dividing point in the road of life where the road branches to the left and to the right. Those who turn to the left, rejecting God's offer of forgiveness of sin and new life in Jesus Christ, march on to their own self-destruction. Those who take the right fork, accepting the graciousness of God through faith and obedience, march on to new life and the ultimate fulfillment of God's purpose of the new person in Christ and the eternal blessing of God.

Thus, the cross of Jesus Christ stands in a prominent, central spot. It stands as the dividing point of history. It stands at the crossroads of life. It stands at the center of our Christian faith. It is in the cross of Jesus Christ that we have the fullest and most dramatic revelation of the forgiving love of God. Apart from the crucifixion of Jesus Christ there would be no salvation. It is no wonder that Paul exclaimed, "For I decided to know nothing among you except Jesus Christ and him crucified" (1 Cor. 2:2).

5
The Redeeming Christ

The most vivid description we have of the life and work of our Savior, Jesus Christ, may be the brief sketch written in the prophecy of Isaiah several hundred years before the time of Jesus. The fifty-third chapter of Isaiah is such a vivid and poignant picture of the suffering of our Savior that it is often read during the observance of the Lord's Supper as though it were written by an eyewitness to the cross. But this remarkable chapter from the Old Testament is not a photograph of what happened to Jesus. It is more like an interpretative portrait done by a sensitive artist who skillfully brings out the details he wishes you to see.

The portrait painted by Isaiah actually includes the last verses of the fifty-second chapter as well as the entire fifty-third chapter (Isa. 52:13 to 53:12). This passage is the fourth in a series of poems in Isaiah dealing with the theme of the Servant of the Lord. The servant poems are shrouded somewhat in mystery. At first it is not clear whom the author is describing. It is not certain just who he is. Only gradually does the picture grow clearer. Indeed, it is not until Jesus has come and the New Testament has been written that it truly becomes clear what was being foretold in the servant poems found in the second part of Isaiah's prophecy. Jesus identified himself with the Servant figure, and as we look at the ministry of Jesus and compare it to what Isaiah wrote in the fifty-third chapter, it becomes clear that the Servant of the Lord is none other than the Messiah. But what a different Messiah he was from what the people had expected. That's why it was only in the New Testament time that it became clear that Isaiah was giving us a vivid description of our suffering Savior.

In Isaiah's picture, Jesus begins in the bleakest kind of insignificance and rises to a place of preeminence. To use Isaiah's graphic words, he was "like a root out of dry ground; he had no form or comeliness that we should look at him, and no beauty that we should desire him" (Isa. 53:2). One would scarcely have expected a root out of a dry ground to amount to anything! From such humble beginnings, Isaiah was saying, one would scarcely expect him to survive at all. It would be more likely that he would wither and vanish, considering his start, than for him to amount to something important. "Can anything good come out of Nazareth?" Nathanael would ask him later (John 1:46).

To the eye of faith he was born in a marvelous, miraculous way, but to the common man, his birth probably looked suspicious at best. In the eyes of many he may have been considered an illegitimate child, born too soon to young parents who were only engaged and not yet married when he was conceived. And the tongues may very well have wagged concerning him, as cruel and unthinking people sometimes charge an innocent child with the sin that brought him into the world.

Though he was born to be King, he wasn't born in royal circumstances, or in a city of royalty. He was born in a borrowed stable into the home of common peasant people. He grew up in Nazareth, a city which evidently had not distinguished itself in any way. He was known as the son of a carpenter and apparently worked at the carpentry trade himself. He evidently was thirty years old before he attracted any kind of attention except for one event in his childhood when he was found asking some precocious questions in the Temple. His life up to the point of his entrance upon his public ministry was evidently rather insignificant. At least there are no traces of him visible to us, except for of one single event.

Even after he began his public ministry, there was not all that much to draw people to him. Oh, at first he was considered a popular preacher—indeed, a prophet after the long prophetic silence of several hundred years. But when the masses found out that he wasn't going to be their kind of Messiah, one who would set up a perpetual bread line like he did when he fed the five thousand from two loaves and five fish, his popularity began to decline. When they realized that he wasn't going to shatter the Roman rule and return Israel to a place of military superiority, his popularity decreased still further. When they found out that he was making stringent demands upon those who wanted to be his followers, there were fewer volunteers to walk with him.

When Jesus showed his revolutionary character in defying rigid regulations that had perverted the real intent of religion and had dehumanized people, the popular sentiment definitely turned against him. Indeed, he was in such conflict with the establishment that the religious leaders of the day began to plot, first to discredit him in the eyes of the people, and when that didn't succeed, to have him killed. The time came when there wasn't much about him that would attract people to him: "He had no form or comeliness that we should look at him, and no beauty that we should desire him" (Isa. 53:2). With the shame, ridicule, and abuse that the people poured out on him before they were through with him at the cross, Isaiah could well describe him,

"As many were astonished at him—
his appearance was so marred, beyond human semblance,
and his form beyond that of the sons of men" (Isa. 52:14).

Isaiah had strained to look forward to the coming Servant of the Lord. He painted a bleak picture of rejection. He saw him as a rejected man, passed over by his contemporaries.

"He was despised and rejected by men;
a man of sorrows, and acquainted with grief;
and as one from whom men hide their faces
he was despised, and we esteemed him not" (53:3).

Isaiah's picture, painted as he strained to look forward hundreds of years, was a precise description of what actually happened. John penned rather sad words to describe Jesus' reception. "He came to his own home, and his own people received him not" (John 1:11).

In his day Jesus was despised by some of the people for the company that he kept. He was ridiculed for being a friend of publicans and harlots, the outcasts of the day.

Jesus may have begun his life in an insignificant way, and he may have been ridiculed by many people in their rejection of him, but that is only part of the story. Most of his ministry lay in a hidden valley, as it were. He descended from the heights where he regularly received the praise and adoration of the angelic choirs and shared the authority of God Almighty in ruling over the universe. On the other side of the valley of suffering and rejection was another peak of grandeur. He was destined for preeminence. This, too, Isaiah foretold. Indeed, this servant poem begins with a description of his exalted glory that should come to him.

"Behold, my servant shall prosper,
he shall be exalted and lifted up,
and shall be very high" (52:13).
As he once was despised and rejected,
"So shall he startle many nations;
kings shall shut their mouths because of him;
for that which has not been told them they shall see,
and that which they have not heard they shall understand" (v. 15).

The New Testament writers proclaimed that Jesus was raised from insignificance to preeminence. Paul declared, "Therefore God has highly exalted him and bestowed on him the name which is above every name, that at the name of Jesus every knee should bow, in heaven and on earth and under the earth, and every tongue confess that Jesus Christ is Lord, to the glory of God the Father" (Phil. 2:9-11). Despised and rejected by men, even crucified on a criminal's cross and buried in a borrowed tomb, nevertheless, God raised him from the clutches of death and exalted him to the heights of glory and authority. Now he has the name which is above every name. God has openly declared him Lord. Millions of people have committed their lives to him. More books have been written about him than any other figure of history. One day he shall return in the final demonstration of his sovereignty as everything is finally brought to honor him as Lord. From insignificance to preeminence, and all as it had been foretold hundreds of years before. And that place of glory and authority was achieved on the pathway of intense suffering.

However Isaiah's portrait of Christ may be read, it must be seen as a portrait of a Suffering Servant of the Lord. The keynote of it all is suffering—the most intense kind of suffering. In a magnificent stroke of understatement, Isaiah described him as "a man of sorrows, and acquainted with grief" (Isa. 53:3). The whole poem is laden with expressions of suffering. "Surely he has borne our griefs and carried our sorrows ... wounded for our transgressions .... He was oppressed, and he was afflicted .... By oppression and judgment he was taken away . . . cut off out of the land of the living . . . . He poured out his soul to death" (vv. 4-5,7-8,12).

Do not assume, however, that he was a helpless victim in all of this sad spectacle of suffering. He was not. His suffering and his death were voluntary. The fact that he suffered at all, much less that he died, is a remarkable fact, considering who he was. He who shared in the formation of the heavens and the earth certainly did not have to suffer. He certainly did not have to submit to shame, ridicule, suffering, and death. They were utterly foreign to his true nature and right. Shortly before his death, as Jesus was teaching his disciples about his coming death, he said, somewhat triumphantly, that he was going the way of the cross because it was the will of the heavenly Father for him to go to the cross, and by the cross he would achieve victory. "For this reason the Father loves me, because I lay down my life, that I may take it again. No one takes it from me, but I lay it down of my own accord. I have power to lay it down, and I have power to take it again; this charge I have received from my Father" (John 10:17-18). Considering that he was the very Son of God, it is a most remarkable thing that he should have taken the way of suffering and death. But he did. It was a voluntary death on that cross.

It would appear to us that he might have gone some other route. He did not have to leave the sanctity of heaven at all. He could have justly left us in our sins. The awful fate that awaited us if he had not come was no more than we deserved as sinners in rebellion against God. Or, if he simply wanted a following, he could have had all the people he could ever have wanted by simply yielding to the desires of the Jews for their own kind of Messiah. In part, this is what the so-called temptation experiences in the wilderness were all about. This was the opportunity that faced him during his ministry when he had to withdraw from the people for a time because he was becoming too popular with them after feeding the five thousand. They were only too willing to proclaim him as their Messiah, but a "Messiah" on their own terms. And this was not at all why Jesus had given up his heavenly glory. He had come for a vastly different purpose.

At the same time, he could have avoided the suffering of the cross. He didn't have to be led away to the slaughter meek as a lamb, as Isaiah put it so graphically. He could have made a show of force—enough force to more than defeat any assault that Satan or his earthly henchmen might have launched. In rebuking Peter for trying to defend him with the sword, he remarked, "Do you think that I cannot appeal to my Father, and he will at once send me more than twelve legions of angels?" (Matt. 26:53). He had not come to establish a kingdom by force.

He could easily have been acquitted. After all, he did not speak a single word of self-defense in his six trials. He made no attempt to have himself freed from those who were bent on his death. Not once did he attempt to set the record straight as he was flagrantly misunderstood by those who made accusations against him. His trials—all six of them—were illegal, even by the standards of that day. His trials were more of a study in lynch-mob tactics than the workings of a court of law, whether civil or religious courts. He was never formally sentenced. His last trial ended when the sitting judge, Pontius Pilate, symbolically washed his hands of the whole matter and bowed out to let the mob have its way.

The point in all this is that he voluntarily chose to die because it suited his purpose. It was this that he had come to do. Any other way would have fallen short of the will of God for him. He saw that his death had a purpose in it. It was to be the fulfillment of his ministry, the climax of what he had come to do. To have stopped short of the cross would have been to miss the very purpose for which he had come to share our lot in the first place. But he did not view his death as forced upon him by a hostile crowd, or an unjust judicial system. He committed himself to the death that he experienced on the cross. The commitment came in the wilderness temptation experience just after his baptism. It was reaffirmed, perhaps, many times during his ministry. Certainly there was a dramatic reaffirmation of his commitment to his death on the cross in his three hours of agonized praying in the garden of Gethsemane just before he was seized and led into the ordeal of his trials and crucifixion.

But he did not die as a martyr, giving himself in behalf of a cause that he could not carry through to completion. He was not a victim but a victor when he died on the cross. He accomplished what he had come to do in the first place. This is why he could say that no man was taking his life from him, that he was laying it down of his own free will. That is why Isaiah could describe him:

"He was oppressed, and he was afflicted,
yet he opened not his mouth;
like a lamb that is led to the slaughter,
and like a sheep that before its shearers is dumb,
so he opened not his mouth" (53:7).

The cross was his grand moment of accomplishment, and he died there willingly. As Isaiah said, "Yet it was the will of the Lord to bruise him" (v. 10). His voluntary death resulted in his exaltation. Isaiah pictures God saying of the Suffering Servant,

"Therefore I will divide him a portion with the great,
and he shall divide the spoil with the strong;
because he poured out his soul to death,
and was numbered with the transgressors" (v. 12).

His death was voluntary, as an acceptance of the will of God for him, but why? What was the purpose in his death on the cross? Again, Isaiah furnishes a striking answer. His death was as a substitute for us.

"Surely he has borne our griefs and carried our sorrows;
yet we esteemed him stricken, smitten by God, and afflicted.
But he was wounded for our transgressions,
he was bruised for our iniquities;
upon him was the chastisement that made us whole,
and with his stripes we are healed" (vv. 4-5).

No human mind can comprehend all that happened at Calvary, but this much is clear: Jesus became our substitute there. Because of what he did there for us we can be freed from sin and its ultimate consequences.

The fact is that God saw us all as guilty sinners, lost in estrangement from him, deserving the worst in punishment. "All we like sheep have gone astray;/we have turned every one to his own way" (v. 6) is the sad assessment of Isaiah. New Testament writers would later drive home the same point. "There is none righteous, no not one . . . . For all have sinned, and come short of the glory of God" (Rom. 3:10,23, KJV). It is the sad fact that the sins of all people led the Father to give his Son as a substitute for us all. The inevitable consequence of sin is death, as God warned from the beginning. But the awful fact is that men have gone right on sinning, succumbing to the murderous plague that has invaded God's creation. But God chose to come to our aid, whether we deserved it or not.

It was the task of the Suffering Servant pictured by Isaiah to take the sufferings of men and the consequences of their sin upon himself. Isaiah saw him as our substitute. "The Lord has laid on him the iniquity of us all" (Isa. 53:6). In the New Testament, Paul expressed it rather simply but forcefully, "But God shows his love for us in that while we were yet sinners Christ died for us" (Rom. 5:8). Jesus Christ, as God's Suffering Servant-Messiah, died for us, on our behalf, as our substitute. This is a recurring theme that is sounded not only in Isaiah but in other portions of the Scriptures as well. "He was cut off out of the land of the living, stricken for the transgression of my people," Isaiah exclaimed (Isa. 53:8).

Following the imagery of the ancient sacrificial system which reminded the Israelites of the seriousness of their sins, Isaiah pictured the Suffering Servant as our sin offering (v. 10). Later, when John the Baptist saw Jesus, John cried, "Behold, the Lamb of God, who takes away the sin of the world!" (John 1:29). Jesus himself linked his sacrificial death on the cross to the forgiveness of sins. As in the Old Testament all important covenants between God and men were sealed with the formal ceremony of sacrifice, so the new covenant that God was making with men for the forgiveness of their sins through Jesus Christ was sealed with a sacrifice. Thus as Jesus instituted the Lord's Supper on the evening before his crucifixion, he offered wine as a symbol of his blood which was going to be shed for others, saying, "This is my blood of the covenant, which is poured out for many for the forgiveness of sins" (Matt. 26:28).

The sacrifice of Jesus Christ upon the cross fills an integral role in the plan of God to provide redemption for us as lost sinners. John declared, "The blood of Jesus his Son cleanses us from all sin" (1 John 1:7). Neither John nor any other Scripture writer tells us exactly how the blood of Jesus cleanses us from our sin, but the inescapable fact is that many Scripture writers declare that the death of Jesus is an essential part of the provision of salvation for us.

The letter to the Hebrews pictures Jesus as the fulfillment of the ancient sacrificial system. Jesus became the ultimate sacrifice, offering himself as the all-sufficient sacrifice which, unlike the previous sacrifices, never needed to be repeated. In building up to the work of Christ, the author of Hebrews refers to the Old Testament, saying, "Without the shedding of blood there is no forgiveness of sins" (Heb. 9:22).

No one can say precisely when or why the custom of sacrifice began. If it began with the command of God, that command is not preserved for us in the Scriptures. We find that both Cain and Abel were bringing sacrifices to the Lord though apparently neither had been commanded to do so. For whatever reason they felt that the proper way to approach God was through the offering of sacrifices. Later, God regulated the practice of sacrifices, giving specific instructions as to the manner of sacrifices. The sacrificial system became a means of instructing the people that they must approach God in obedience and faith. The sacrificial system took on an educational significance. But no one can say precisely how sacrifices "worked" in the provision of salvation, or precisely what the significance of sacrifices was. It is not certain whether the essence of sacrifice was the presentation of a prescribed gift to God, or whether it was the symbolic presentation of a life to God. Some have felt that the sacrifices were of a penal character, with the victim suffering the penalty deserved by the one offering the sacrifice, but that cannot be substantiated from Scripture, especially when it is remembered that provision was made for other kinds of sacrifices to be offered instead of a blood offering when a proper sacrificial animal was not available.

But the point in all of this is that the death of Jesus on the cross was seen as the logical fulfillment of the sacrificial system itself. It was seen as essential to our salvation. In terms of the ancient system it was declared that his blood has an essential part in cleansing us from sin. Somehow God used the sacrifice of his Son upon the cross to result in our salvation. And this was part of the interpretation that Isaiah gave to the work of the Suffering Servant hundreds of years before the time of Jesus. Isaiah saw Jesus as making himself an offering for sin, resulting in the salvation of many (Isa. 53:10-11). Though we may not understand precisely how the death of Jesus in our behalf was essential to our salvation, the fact is that the Scripture writers viewed his sacrifice as essential without telling us just how.

The ancient system of sacrifice for the sins of the people was at best no more than an educational tool pointing the people to the grace of God which forgives and takes away our sins. It was no more than an interim arrangement whereby the worshiper could gain some assurance of having approached God with the burden of sins to find release from guilt. The writer of Hebrews observes that the ancient sacrificial system was at best only provisional and inadequate. "For it is impossible that the blood of bulls and goats should take away sins" (10:4). But somehow, what Jesus has done is sufficient to bring to man once and for all the forgiveness of sins. If the sacrificial system had been pointing forward to Christ all along, as some would maintain, after Christ there is no longer any need for a sacrifice of any kind. Jesus has once and for all offered the sacrifice that is beyond price and which cannot be repeated. "For by a single offering he has perfected for all time those who are sanctified" (Heb. 10:14).

In the analogy of the sacrificial system, Jesus worked out our salvation for us not only as the offering above all price, but functioned for us in the role of the great High Priest and he continues to function in our behalf as a great High Priest, making intercession for us before the Father. His blood was essential for our salvation, but it is the whole person of Jesus who provides our salvation. It is through his whole person that Jesus as the Suffering Servant pictured by Isaiah brings us redemption. Whatever our shortcomings may have been, what Jesus did in his life and in his death on the cross has made up for them. Whatever penalties we may have incurred, Jesus has satisfied any demands of the law in our behalf.

Isaiah saw so pointedly that the whole process of the suffering and death of Jesus was intimately related to our sinful predicament. It was because of our pitiful condition that Jesus as God's Suffering Servant was so pathetically afflicted.

"Surely he has borne our griefs and carried our sorrows;
yet we esteemed him stricken, smitten by God, and afflicted.
But he was wounded for our transgressions,

he was bruised for our iniquities; upon him was the chastisement that made us whole,

and with his stripes we are healed" (Isa. 53:4-5).

Several elements stand out pointedly in this moving description of the suffering of Jesus. One thing is that he bore our sins upon himself. Somehow he so identified himself with us in his love for us that he took upon himself the load that he saw descending upon ourselves in the calamity that we were experiencing in our sinful rejection of God. Peter described our Lord in much the same way as he later looked back to Jesus rather than forward as did Isaiah. "He himself bore our sins in his own body on the tree, that we might die to sin and live to righteousness. By his wounds you have been healed" (1 Pet. 2:24). This was an apparent reference to Isaiah's beautiful passage.

Notice also that Jesus was not only bearing our sins in his own body, but we are experiencing the death of Jesus in a vicarious experience. In a vicarious experience one person may so identify with the experience of another that he may share the other person's experience in spirit. Thus when Jesus died on the cross for me, I shared in that death by dying to sin in myself. Indeed, Paul stresses the urgency of that vicarious suffering with Christ. He described Christians as "heirs of God and fellow heirs with Christ, *provided we suffer with him in order that we may also be glorified with him*" (Rom. 8:17, italics added for emphasis).

Elsewhere, Paul emphasizes this vicarious relationship of the believer to the suffering of Christ saying, "We were buried therefore with him by baptism into death, so that as Christ was raised from the dead by the glory of the Father, we too might walk in newness of life" (Rom. 6:4). This close relationship that must exist between the Christian and the Savior is further stressed by Paul in another place. "I have been crucified with Christ; it is no longer I who live, but Christ who lives in me; and the life I now live in the flesh I live by faith in the Son of God who loved me and gave himself for me" (Gal. 2:20).

We share not only the death of Christ through a vicarious experience, but we also share in the results of his death. His death was a victory for him. And his death has a healing effect upon our sin-sick souls. Isaiah said this when he said, "Upon him was the chastisement that made us whole, and with his stripes we are healed" (Isa. 53:5). The sacrificial sufferings of Jesus form a healing balm that cures the soul that is sick unto death. Isaiah's language is graphic. The stripes off the back of Jesus become threads of love to bind up the broken, gaping wounds in our lives.

On the cross Jesus not only took our place but he did something for us that we could not do for ourselves. We could have suffered on the cross the same as he did. And we would have deserved it where he did not. But there was no way that we might have achieved healing for our sin-sick souls. Only the divine power of God could do that. It had to be done for us, since we could not do it for ourselves. Perhaps this is the very heart of the work of Jesus upon the cross. He not only was a substitute for us in whom we experienced death vicariously. He opened to us healing for the worst of all afflictions, the fatal malady of sin. "By his stripes we are healed!" A favorite gospel song says it beautifully, "There is a balm in Gilead to heal the sin-sick soul."

Hundreds of years after Isaiah the apostle Paul said the same thing, though somewhat differently. "Therefore, if anyone is in Christ, he is a new creation; the old has passed away, behold, the new has come" (2 Cor. 5:17).

Isaiah gave us a very moving portrait of our Suffering Savior. He was meek and lowly, rising from insignificance to preeminence. He died a paradoxical, voluntary death. He died a substitutionary death, taking our sins and sorrows upon himself. And his awful death and hideous sufferings somehow have a tremendous healing power as they are applied to us. We experience death to sin in him in a vicarious experience. We share in his marvelous life. Indeed, he becomes life for us as he makes himself our substitute. Because he left heaven, we have the promise of eternal life in heaven. Because he died, we can live. And all of this is because of the cross. Nowhere is the pathos of the Suffering Savior and his cross more movingly portrayed than in the vivid picture painted by Isaiah. And that makes it all the more remarkable, since it was painted with moving words and vivid expressions hundreds of years before the time of Jesus Christ who came as the living fulfillment of Isaiah's prophecy.

6
It Is Finished

The scene on the hill of Calvary was a touching, tragic one. Crucifixion was a crude and cruel form of death. Merciful death usually came only at the end of a long period of agony. It often took twenty-four to forty-eight hours, and sometimes more, for death to claim its victim. Merely to contemplate the awfulness of the suffering endured by one who was crucified is to endure a special kind of mental anguish for a sensitive soul.

Think of the agony that must have been shared by the family and followers of Jesus as they stood by helpless and bewildered that day when Jesus was crucified. They must have been nearly shattered themselves as they watched in horror at what was taking place.

Merciful death came swiftly for Jesus that black day. And it was a black day, figuratively. Here, on that day, the most heinous of all crimes was enacted, the crucifixion of the Son of God. The very Son of God, who had renounced heaven and all of his heavenly prerogatives of sitting at the right hand of the Father, was now being put to death in what was tantamount to a lynching party. It was literally a black day, for the sun refused to shine and the earth was darkened for awhile on that fateful Friday as Jesus hung on the cross. The earth itself was convulsed with the tremor of an earthquake. And the giant curtain, the veil of the Temple that kept all but the high priest out of the most sacred part of the Temple, symbolizing the presence of God, was torn asunder to indicate that no longer was man shut away from God.

Merciful death came quickly to Jesus that day, perhaps because he was already weakened from a long night of beatings and abuse before he was ever nailed to the cross. Or perhaps God released him from his sufferings sooner than might have been expected because he saw his purpose fulfilled and could stand the awful scene no longer himself.

While Jesus was hanging on the cross, he called out seven times, according to the gospel writers. Three times were in concern for others. He cried out the first time, "Father, forgive them; for they know not what they do" (Luke 23:34). His concern was not for himself but for those who had just pounded the great spikes through his hands and feet. His concern was for those who had shouted in mob action for his death.

His second word was the word of acceptance to the repentant thief who was crucified alongside him. His third utterance was his commitment of his mother to the care of his beloved disciple, John.

The other four cries from Jesus as he hung on the cross had reference to himself. There was the cry of anguished desolation, when for a brief moment it seemed to him that even God his Father had forsaken him. As the weary day wore on there was the cry of physical suffering when he cried out in thirst.

When his six hours on the cross were about over and death was at hand, he cried out, "It is finished" (John 19:30). His last words were to say, with a loud voice, "Father, into thy hands I commit my spirit!" (Luke 23:46). He may have wavered in anguish and uncertainty a little while earlier when he cried out, "My God, my God, why hast thou forsaken me?" (Matt. 27:46). But in the end he knew full well that he was not forsaken. For his last words were a sweet release from earthly anguish and suffering as he slipped into the loving, waiting hands of his heavenly Father who had been hovering nearby all the while.

But what of that cry, "It is finished" (John 19:30)? What did he mean? What did the milling crowd think? What did the various groups of people think as he uttered these words in what was almost his last gasp of breath? Indeed, as John recorded the events of the closing moments of the life of Jesus, these were his last words. What did he mean?

Many of the people on the hill of Calvary that day were simply curiosity seekers. They had heard the sound of the mob that was shouting for Jesus' death and had fallen into the procession winding its way out of the city of Jerusalem toward the hill of the skull,

Golgotha, where public executions were held. They had no real interest in what was going on. They had only come along for the show. So, when they heard him exclaim, "It is finished," they simply understood him to be saying that the show was over. They understood only that his suffering had come to an end. The agony of hanging suspended from great spikes driven through hands and feet had finally come to its merciful conclusion. A good bit sooner than normally expected, but now that poor fellow was out of his misery. That is probably all that they understood in that cry from the cross.

There was more to the message than that, however. For Jesus those words were no mere words of resignation to his fate as he recognized that the final moment of his life had come. They meant something more to him. In fact, they were the key to understanding his cross.

His followers who were in the crowd missed the point, however. Perhaps they should be excused for not understanding, for they were in a state of shock. They really did not know what was happening. True, Jesus had been telling them for months that he would be crucified by the Jewish establishment, but they never really were able to accept that; and, when it finally happened, they were profoundly shocked. They were frightened as they stood in the crowd on Calvary that day. Only a little earlier one of those closest to Jesus, Simon Peter, had sworn with an oath that he did not even know Jesus. As a matter of fact, we do not know for certain that any of the twelve were so much as in the crowd that day, with the exception of John, to whom Jesus committed the care of his mother.

Those of his followers who had dared to go to the scene of the crucifixion that day must certainly have been bewildered. They thought that they had seen the power of God at work in him. Simon Peter had spoken for the group in confessing him to be the Messiah. But none of them had understood what it meant to be the Messiah. It was not until after the cross and the resurrection that they came to understand what it meant to be the Messiah, the Savior. All they could think of then was that all of their hopes and dreams had been shattered by those final words, "It is finished."

This was the death knell of all that they had hoped for in Jesus.

They had hoped that he would be the Messiah to bring to fruition all of the nationalistic dreams that they had had for Israel. They had longed for a return of the glory of David's day. Some of them had left everything they had to follow Jesus when he summoned them by the Sea of Galilee. Jesus had summoned them to be fishers of men, but they did not quite know what that meant. However, they did sense something special about Jesus and they were all too ready to cast their lot with him. Indeed, two of them had been all too ready to sit at his left and right hand in places of authority!

"It is finished" were the saddest words that the followers of Jesus had ever heard. To them they were the words that meant that all of their hopes and dreams were shattered. Their lives had just fallen apart and now they would have to try to pick up the pieces and start over again. The death of Jesus simply meant to them his defeat, and their own defeat. Only they had been lucky. At least, they survived; Jesus had suffered an unspeakable fate. It was not until he was raised from the dead that they saw how they had missed the point of what Jesus had been trying to tell them for months. Indeed, the resurrection came as quite a shock to them. It was only then that they understood what Jesus had been trying to tell them.

The scribes and Pharisees who heard Jesus cry, "It is finished," saw it differently. Indeed, they welcomed that cry with a curious glee. This was a cry of victory to them, *their own victory*. For they had been plotting the death of Jesus for a long time. When Jesus uttered those words, "It is finished," the scribes and Pharisees took it as a signal that they were finally rid of that hated troublemaker. From early in the life of Jesus, the scribes and Pharisees had been set against him in bitter opposition. Jesus might have said that he had come not to break the law but to fulfill the law, but the Pharisees understood very clearly that on any terms Jesus meant the end of the Judaistic system as they knew it. And they weren't going to give up without a fight. At first they tried to discredit Jesus in the eyes of the people with tricky questions and with accusations against him for the company that he kept with publicans and harlots, among others. And it was not long until they realized that it would take more than public embarrassment to get rid of Jesus.

They actively plotted his death. They tried to have him arrested more than once and even took up stones to kill him on one occasion.

When Jesus uttered those words from the cross, "It is finished," the Jewish establishment heard them as a signal of victory for their cause. Now they were through with that troublemaker. And after the example that had been made of him it would be a long time before anyone would dare to challenge their authority again.

The scribes and Pharisees could not have been more wrong, however. The cry of Jesus, "It is finished," was no admission of defeat. It was no resignation from a lost cause. Even though the scribes and Pharisees had long tried to bring about his death, Jesus did not see himself as a victim or as a martyr. Jesus had said, long before the cross, "I lay down my life, that I may take it again. No one takes it from me, but I lay it down of my own accord. I have power to take it again; this charge I have received from my Father" (John 10:17-18). When Peter was ready to defend Jesus with the sword as Jesus was seized at the betrayal in the garden, Jesus told Peter that he needed no defense. Jesus said that even then he could call upon his Father who would send twelve legions of angels to defend him against this little clandestine party who had come to seize him like a common criminal. But that would not fulfill his purpose. Somehow Jesus saw in the cross what no one else was able to see until the whole dreadful drama was over.

Jesus said, in his last moment on the cross, "It is finished." The curious crowd saw in this only the end of his suffering. The followers of Jesus saw only the dashing of their hopes. The Pharisees saw only the defeat of Jesus in their own victory over him. But they were all wrong. None of them understood what Jesus said when he exclaimed, "It is finished."

What then, did Jesus mean? This was his shout of victory, no meek sigh of defeat or somber moan of resignation. This was his shout of victory, the recognition of the fulfillment of his purpose. He had not been unaware of the opposition of the scribes and Pharisees and their plots to do away with him. Indeed, he knew that this was part of the price that he must pay in order to fulfill God's purpose for his earthly life. He could not bring in God's salvation short of the supreme sacrifice of himself on the cross. So, when his moment of death came, he welcomed it as the signal of his accomplishment of his purpose.

The closing words of Jesus from the cross, "It is finished," simply meant that Jesus recognized that he had completed the process of salvation which had been begun thousands of years before. From the time of the first sin of the first pair upon the earth in the Garden of Eden, God had been moving toward that moment when he would lay bare his redeeming love in the most dramatic way possible, through the death of his own Son. Now that process was fulfilled. Jesus saw that the whole of redemptive history had come to a focus in him.

To Jesus, the cross was not the sign of his defeat. He viewed it as the crowning achievement of his life. Though family and followers alike had tried to turn him away from his date with seeming disaster in Jerusalem, he would not budge one inch from his determination to drink the bitter cup of suffering to the very end in his pursuit of salvation for a lost world. The cross was no defeat for him. It was the signal of the crowning achievement of his life.

"It is finished." Now, in Jesus, the perfect life had been lived. Never before had the world seen what authentic human life was like. The first man upon the earth had sinned and had missed God's purpose for his life. And the story of Adam and his defection from God is the story of every other man who has ever lived. But in Jesus, there is the perfect display of righteousness and love, united in a beautiful expression of godliness. And now for all who have lived since that time, the life of Jesus Christ is held forth as the pristine example that each of us should copy.

Remember, if you will, that the life of Jesus is no artificial example. His life was lived out under the same kinds of conditions, the same kinds of temptations and problems that you face. But his life, though thoroughly human like ours, was marked by a complete dedication to the will of the heavenly Father. What we could not do, he fully accomplished in living out a life that was unstained by sin. Never once did an evil word come from his lips. Never once did his foot follow a wrong path in life. Never once did his life set a wrong example. Never once did his mind harbor a wicked thought.

Even more significantly, Jesus' life was always marked by the positive qualities of love, goodness, righteousness, and compassion. He demonstrated complete concern for his fellow human beings. He always portrayed complete dedication to the will of his Father. In Jesus Christ the perfect life had been lived. This is one of the prerequisites of his being our Savior. If he had been less than perfect, he too would have needed a Savior. As the author of the letter to the Hebrews recognized, in terms of the ancient sacrificial system, Jesus, as the sacrificial lamb of God, had to be perfect if he was to save us and put an end to the oft-repeated sacrifices which really could not save anyhow.

"It is finished." Jesus was saying that the perfect sacrifice for sin had now been made. For centuries, the Jewish people had brought their sacrifices as part of the ritual prescribed for their obtaining salvation. It was God's way of teaching them that salvation came on God's terms, not man's. The offering of a blood sacrifice had been an integral part of the process of salvation for hundreds of years. Now, the death of Jesus marked the end of that process of sacrifice. Jesus offered the once-for-all sacrifice that need not be repeated; he was the fulfillment of the sacrificial system. The author of the letter to the Hebrews reminds us, "Indeed, under the law almost everything is purified with blood, and without the shedding of blood there is no forgiveness of sins" (9:22). Jesus declared, shortly before his death, as he observed the Lord's Supper with the disciples, "This is my blood of the covenant, which is poured out for many for the forgiveness of sins" (Matt. 26:28).

Once the high priest could enter the holy of holies in the Temple only once a year, bearing the blood of a sacrificial offering. Now, the way into the very presence of God is opened for all through Christ Jesus. "Therefore, brethren, since we have confidence to enter the sanctuary by the blood of Jesus, by the new and living way which he opened for us through the curtain, that is, through his flesh, and since we have a great priest over the house of God, let us draw near with a true heart in full assurance of faith" (Heb. 10:19-22).

Not only did Jesus offer the perfect sacrifice for us, he also became the perfect high priest for us. All that the Old Testament sacrificial system with its appointed priests and offerings had

attempted to do for us has now been brought to glorious fulfillment in Christ Jesus. We have a perfect high priest who is our
representative seated at the right hand of God the Father to make
intercession for us always. He knows our problems and needs
firsthand, for he has been one of us and has walked in our shoes.
As God's Son he so completely identified with us that he made
the ultimate sacrifice for us so that there is no longer need for sacrifices for our sins. He now offers forgiveness openly and freely to
all who come in repentance and faith.

"It is finished." The love of God for sinful men has now been
revealed to the fullest extent possible. No greater display of love
can be offered than what has been given us in the cross of Jesus
Christ. When Jesus had poured out his life on the cross, the
depths of the love of God for sinful men was made crystal clear.
There is no sacrifice too great for God to make in an attempt to
save us. As Jesus said, "Greater love has no man than this, that a
man lay down his life for his friends" (John 15:13). And remember, it is not for righteous men that God sent his son to die. It was
for sinners—sinners of all kinds, murderers, liars, adulterers,
thieves, hypocrites. But as Paul said, this is the genius of the love
of God for us. "God shows his love for us in that while we were yet
sinners Christ died for us" (Rom. 5:8).

The best-known verse in the Bible stresses this love which impelled God to send his Son into our world to save us. "For God so
loved the world that he gave his only Son, that whoever believes
in him should not perish but have eternal life" (John 3:16). The
love of God for man is a self-giving love that simply knows no
limit. No sacrifice is too great for God in his attempt to reach fallen
sinners. God did not stop short of sacrificing his Son, even in
death. So, Jesus came to live among us, as one of us, even at the
cost of his death on our behalf, to convey the forgiving love of
God for us. It is no wonder, then, that when Jesus came to the last
moments of his life, he exclaimed, "It is finished." Nothing more
could be done or said to emphasize the sacrificial love of God for
those of us who were perishing in our sins. The love of God has
been revealed in the supreme example of love, an example that
ought to startle every soul and convict every conscience.

"It is finished." What else did Jesus mean? We have not yet

drained the words of their meaning. He was also saying that the mortal enemies of sin and death had been vanquished. Jesus viewed his cross as the defeat of the powers that had seduced and enslaved man. It might seem paradoxical that as he gasped his last breath he was proclaiming his victory. But he knew that death could not hold him. He knew that his death would ultimately mean the death of death itself and the undoing of the power of sin. He had faced all of the temptations that Satan could muster and defeated them all. Jesus said of his ministry, "Now is the judgment of this world, now shall the ruler of this world be cast out; and I, when I am lifted up from the earth, will draw all men to myself" (John 12:31-32).

Jesus saw his death as the defeat of sin and Satan. And as Paul looked back on the cross and the resurrection, he could exult,
"Death is swallowed up in victory.
O death, where is thy victory?
O death, where is thy sting?
The sting of death is sin, and the power of sin is the law. But thanks be to God, who gives us the victory through our Lord Jesus Christ" (1 Cor. 15:54-57).

Through Jesus' work on the cross for us, death need not hold sway any longer. Jesus has defeated this enemy in a stunning victory that publishes to all the world the saving power of God.

"It is finished." Through Jesus Christ the way has been opened into life. Not only has the power of death been broken, and the power of sin destroyed, Jesus has opened the way into life. "Truly, truly, I say to you, he who hears my word and believes him who sent me, has eternal life; he does not come into judgment, but has passed from death to life" (John 5:24). Or, as he said on another occasion, "Whoever drinks of the water that I shall give him will never thirst; the water that I shall give him will become in him a spring of water welling up to eternal life" (John 4:14).

Now, because of the liberating, regenerating power of God through Jesus Christ, human life can be lived on another plane. There is another dimension of life which would not be possible apart from Jesus Christ and his cross. The cross was a cruel instrument of death to Jesus Christ, but to us it is a life-giving instrument. Were it not for the cross, Jesus could not say, "I came that they may have life and have it abundantly" (John 10:10). And Jesus himself is the door into that life. Apart from him there cannot be that abundant life. As Jesus said, "I am the door; if any one enters by me, he will be saved, and will go in and out and find pasture" (John 10:9). Jesus, as the good shepherd, is the door to eternal life. And he is essential to that good life, that eternal life. Apart from his cross, he could not offer that new life. Somehow, the cross was part of the path that Jesus had to follow to come to the point of offering to be the door into life eternal. So, it is no wonder that Jesus exclaimed, "It is finished," when he came to the last moments of his life on the cross.

All of that—at least that much—is implicit in the victory cry of Jesus from the cross. He saw the cross as the supreme accomplishment of his life. Others on Calvary that day missed the significance of what he was saying. They had various interpretations, depending on their own personal situations. Some saw it only as welcome relief to cruel suffering; some as defeat of all of their fond hopes and dreams; still others as a victory for their own devious plans. But, from the cross, Jesus saw it as his victory. From heaven God saw it as the accomplishment of his plan of redemption which he had been unfolding from the beginning of human history.

The only question that remains is what that cry, "It is finished," means to us today. Our perspective on the cross is crucial. We desperately need to perceive its deeper significance. It is to our own harm if we, like the crowd at Calvary, see it only from a superficial or selfish perspective. Our attitude to the gospel of the cross determines our lives, both here and now and in the eternity beyond this world. God has done all that he can in attempting to reach us by giving his son as the source of the gospel of redeeming love. Beyond this God cannot go. That does not mean that God put Jesus on the cross and then has rested since. Far from it! He has been at work ever since trying, through the Holy Spirit, to woo and convict lost souls and lead them to salvation. But God has taken the supreme step in trying to reach us through the cross. All of the message of salvation is now a message intimately bound up with the cross. The cross is central to the gospel of salvation. It is the hub around which all of the rest of the Christian message revolves. Remove that cross and what is left falls into a meaningless shamble of bits and pieces of religious ideas and symbols—a religious jumble without central meaning and without saving power.

So Jesus exclaimed in victory, "It is finished." He had done the most that God could do. But the work goes on—the work of proclaiming the victory of the cross to all people. How they receive that message depends on who they are and where they are in life. To all who find redemption through the message of the crucified Savior there is a common experience of trust in the one who died on that cross. There is a common element of his entrance into their lives through the indwelling presence of the Holy Spirit. But there are also some differences.

Paul was an archenemy of the Christian people of the first century. He was convinced that Jesus Christ was not the long-promised Messiah. He could not see that the cross could play any part in the hope of the chosen people for salvation. Consequently, he became a persecutor of the church. And he must have been a pretty good one at that. He was given authority to enlarge his circle of persecution to include Damascus as well as the environs of Jerusalem. As he was traveling the highway from Jerusalem toward Damascus, he had a dramatic experience that changed his whole life. He suddenly found himself confronted with the thing that he least expected: the living presence of the Lord Jesus Christ himself.

Paul fell to the ground blinded by a dazzling light. Who knows what brought on this encounter. Perhaps even as his heart was filled with hatred for the Christians he was seeking he was remembering the pitiful scene of the death of Stephen, the first Christian martyr. Paul had been present at that gory scene where Stephen was stoned to death because of his testimony to Jesus Christ. In fact, Paul may well have been in a position of authority at that awful scene. Those who stoned Stephen laid their garments at the feet of Paul while they were carrying out their foul deed.

Now Paul lay on the ground blinded by a light far brighter than the noonday sun. He heard a voice calling to him. When Paul responded with a plea, "Who are you Lord?" the shocking answer came back, "I am Jesus, whom you are persecuting" (Acts 9:5).

Paul was instructed to go on to Damascus, when he inquired what he must do. He then became the archpromoter of Christianity, its foremost preacher and theologian. His was a dramatic experience with the Christ of the cross. This dramatic experience made a radical difference in his life. He was revolutionized by his encounter with Jesus on the Damascus road. This experience made such a profound impression upon Paul that his whole life was then ordered around the cross. He later told the Corinthians, words he could equally well have addressed to any audience, "For I decided to know nothing among you except Jesus Christ and him crucified" (1 Cor. 2:2). And to him that meant what he said in Galatians 2:20, "I have been crucified with Christ; it is no longer I who live, but Christ who lives in me; and the life I now live in the flesh I live by faith in the Son of God, who loved me and gave himself for me."

On the other hand, this writer had an entirely different kind of encounter with the Christ of the cross. My experience of salvation was not the Damascus road type. My experience of salvation through faith in Jesus Christ came when I was an eight-year-old boy. As far back as I can remember, when I was a little child my mother took time daily to read the Bible to me and pray with me. I shall never forget one special day when we had our devotions together. She very carefully told me the old familiar story of the cross of Jesus Christ. She explained to me that this was God's way of bearing my sin—explaining to me that even as an eight-year-old boy I, too, had done things wrong in the eyes of God and that I would continue to displease God as I grew older. She explained to me that the cross was God's way of offering forgiveness of my sins and eternal life through his Son, Jesus Christ.

I shall never forget her asking me if I felt that I needed to ask God to forgive me. I shall never forget her asking me if I wanted to accept Jesus Christ as my Savior. As she explained that the cross was for me, too, I just could not refuse. Quietly, at the side of my bed, by my mother, I prayed a simple prayer of faith, asking God to come into my life. That was as much a turning point in my life as the Damascus road encounter was for Paul. Yes, there were some profound differences in our experiences. I had not persecuted anyone. I had not committed some of the "worse" sins of the flesh. I had not led a wicked life. I was just beginning to understand a few things about what life is all about.

But there were some striking similarities. I too tried to make the cross of Jesus Christ central in my life. I too tried to identify myself with the Christ who died on the cross for me. Jesus exclaimed, "It is finished." His part was completed that day on the cross as the work of God in redemption came to a crucial climax. The cross was the end for Jesus, the goal that he was pursuing. But for me, and countless others like me, it was only the beginning. For now I must say with Paul, in the midst of the Christian life: "One thing I do, forgetting what lies behind and straining forward to what lies ahead, I press on toward the goal for the prize of the upward call of God in Christ Jesus" (Phil. 3:13-14).

The cross, then, stands at the center of the Christian faith and life. For Jesus, the climax of his earthly life. For me, the motive of my life. And in both instances, the power and love of God laid bare.

7

There Were Three Crosses

There were three crosses on Golgotha. The supreme significance of the one in the middle makes us tend to forget the other two. But the other two crosses help us to remember why the one in the middle was so important. In fact, the two common criminals who were crucified at the right and left of Jesus are a very pointed study in the crucial importance of our reaction to the central cross where Jesus Christ, the Son of God, was pouring out his life to redeem men who are lost in their sins.

The three crosses on Calvary made a pathetic scene for the carnival-like mob to view. Public executions of any kind are horrible to contemplate, at least to the modern mind. But the horrors of a public crucifixion of three men go beyond comprehension.

As Jesus hung on the central cross the soldiers who had nailed him to the cross gambled for his garments, possibly all of the earthly possessions that he had. In the crowd of people about those three crosses that day there were at least a few who were numb with shock and grief. There was certainly Jesus' mother. For, as he hung on the cross, with death fast approaching, he committed her to the care of his beloved disciple, John, who was also there. There may well have been others of his followers in the crowd around the three crosses, but the Scripture writers give us no hint as to how many or who they were. By the time Jesus died, there were at least some who asked for his body so that they might give it a decent, if hasty, burial. The beginning of the Jewish sabbath was at hand and they did not have time for a burial fitting for their Master. Little did they know that he wasn't going to stay in the tomb but three short days and nights! Oh, how he had tried to tell them, but they just couldn't understand. Not until it was all over on Easter morning.

The cross in the center usually claims our attention when we look at Calvary. But the other two crosses have a message for us, too. In a sense they are the reason why there was a cross in the middle. These other two crosses represented two opposite reactions to the cross in the center—two kinds of reactions that we still see today.

One of those other two who were crucified seemed to join the scoffing crowd. He railed, "Are you not the Christ? Save yourself and us!" (Luke 23:39). He really had no idea who this was dying on the cross next to his. He simply joined the shouting mob as it taunted Jesus. How little did he know! What an opportunity he missed!

On the cross on the other side of Jesus it was a different story. Somehow this poor fellow sensed that something very unusual was taking place on that center cross. Indeed, he rebuked his companion in crime for taunting Jesus and then made an earnest plea to the man on the center cross. "Jesus, remember me when you come into your kingdom" (v. 42). And he received the welcome reply, "Truly, I say to you, today you will be with me in Paradise" (v. 43).

One sinner was lost at the gates of heaven and one sinner was saved at the gates of hell. And that is the way it has been ever since Calvary. The reaction of persons to the cross in the center at Calvary has sealed their eternal destiny. Some have found the cross to be their eternal condemnation and some have found the cross to be their eternal salvation.

One sinner lost at the gates of heaven! He never really knew what was happening at Calvary. He died as he apparently lived, superficial and sarcastic. He was being executed for some crime or another. Matthew's Gospel says that he was a thief, as was his companion. It really doesn't matter what crime he had committed. There were many crimes that were punishable by death at that time. He was being executed justly, or so his companion in crime who was being executed along with him said. And, from a spiritual perspective, he was getting the rewards for his wayward life. He, like all men, was a sinner. There was no question about that. For, the Scriptures tell us that all men are sinners (Rom. 3:23) and that the wages of sin is death (6:23). Any man who spends his life in the pursuit of sin can be quite sure that he is only paving the way to his own destruction. The apostle Paul spelled out a spiritual axiom quite clearly, one that all men should hear. "Do not be deceived; God is not mocked, for whatever a man sows, that he will also reap. For he who sows to his own flesh will from the flesh reap corruption; but he who sows to the Spirit will from the Spirit reap eternal life" (Gal. 6:7-8).

This man hanging on a cross alongside Jesus had the opportunity of a lifetime, if he could just have recognized it. The central event of all time was unfolding in his very presence—and he missed its significance. Here he was alongside the Son of God to whom he could have pleaded for mercy, as did his companion in crime. He was at the threshold of heaven and did not realize it. He was inadvertently a part of the drama to which the prophets had pointed toward for hundreds of years. He was in the midst of the scene to which the Christian world has looked back in loving reverence for nearly two thousand years. He was on the very spot where God was laying bare his redeeming grace for just such despicable sinners as he was. And all that he could do was utter a sarcastic taunt at the Son of God.

To those of us who have found that the cross is the power of God to save and transform wicked lives, it is unthinkable that one could be so close to salvation and still reject it. Yet, it happens all the time. Many men are lost, seemingly at the very gates of heaven. They have heard the gospel over and over. Many have witnessed to them earnestly. Many have prayed for them daily. The Holy Spirit has tugged at their hearts trying to get them to forsake their sin and turn to Jesus. They have had a lifetime of opportunities to receive Jesus Christ as Lord of their lives and receive the redemption wrought out on the cross. But their stubborn hearts have refused to yield to the very end. They were lost at the gates of heaven, so close, but so far.

This one who died at Jesus' side, resolute in his sin, could blame no one but himself for his eternal loss. Indeed, he may well have had less excuse for being lost than has any other man in hell. For he saw firsthand what took place on Calvary. He made his choice and stuck with it. Perhaps he was like the rich man Jesus told about. He was so wrapped up in his selfishness, enjoying the good things of this life, that he was oblivious to the poor beggar, Lazarus, who laid daily at his gate in starvation and suffering. His hard heart cut him off from God for eternity. Many a man has lived this life in such hardheartedness, refusing to let God into any part of his life, and has thus sent himself into eternity lost, beyond the reach of God's mercy forever.

God sends no one to hell. Men send themselves when they refuse the grace God offers them. They send themselves when they choose to spend their lives in selfishness and sinful rebellion against the will of God. Someone has said if any man goes to hell he has to crawl over the grace of God to get there. So it was with this man who died at the side of Jesus on Calvary that day. So close, but so far from salvation.

This poor fellow who lost a beautiful opportunity to be saved ought to be a lesson to everyone who reads his pathetic story. Just being close to salvation is not enough. One must actually experience it for himself in a personal act of faith before the message of the cross can do him any good. Just being close, or just having good intentions about being saved, is not enough. I once knew a man who had symptoms of a serious heart disorder. His doctor urged him to enter the hospital immediately for extensive tests. But he thought he was too busy just then and could put it off a little while. A few days later he was on his way to see a friend who was ill in the very hospital where he would undergo tests in a few weeks. As he walked up the steps into the lobby, he dropped dead with a massive heart attack. So close, but so far.

One can stand next door to heaven and still be lost. If the poor criminal on the cross at the side of Jesus did not prove that, then Judas Iscariot did. For Judas was a man who had the opportunity to be in the inner circle of those about Jesus during virtually the whole of Jesus' public ministry. But Judas apparently never did really understand who Jesus was and what he had come to do. As Jesus was coming to the climax of his earthly ministry, Judas betrayed him for a mere thirty pieces of silver. And when Judas came to his senses just a little while later, he realized what a golden opportunity he had missed—and went and hanged himself. So close but so far.

Judas and the nameless criminal on the cross were not the only ones who had been so close and still missed it, however. There was the rich young ruler who once came to Jesus. He professed to a good moral life, keeping all of the law (at least in his own eyes). Jesus told him that all he lacked was the faith to sell all that he had, give it to the poor, and then follow him. But riches stood between him and the kind of unfettered commitment that Jesus was asking of him. His riches stood between him and the kingdom of God. There were numerous others who found various reasons—excuses, really—for not yielding to the call of Jesus. They were represented by Jesus as those who had to wait for a more convenient time—"I must first bury my aging father." "I must try my new yoke of oxen." "I have married a new wife and can't come right now." Some can be so close, but so far. And such superficial things keep them from salvation. What a tragic loss they suffer when they lose heaven itself.

One of the three crosses marked the death of a man who turned his back on a golden opportunity to receive a full pardon from his many sins and the gift of eternal life. True, he did not deserve it—but neither has any other man who has ever received the free gift of salvation. Jesus did not die for the righteous and deserving. He died for the unrighteous, unlovely, sinful outcasts of this world. He cast his lot with them, not the "good" people of the religious establishment of his day. He even died as one of the outcasts, with them on the middle cross on Calvary that day. And in that fateful time while Jesus hung on that central cross one of his companions in crucifixion opened his heart in faith and one gave a last display of his hardheartedness. One was saved at the gates of hell and one was lost at the very gates of heaven.

On the cross at the other side of Jesus was a man who showed for all time that it is never too late to turn to God in faith. He was a man who was dying for crimes that he had committed. He really had no excuse to offer. In fact, he felt that what was happening to him was only just—he felt that because of his crimes he deserved death. He recognized that the only injustice being done that day on Calvary was the crucifixion of the one who was hanging on the cross in the center. As his companion in crime taunted Jesus, this man rebuked him, saying, "Do you not fear God, since you are under the same sentence of condemnation? And we indeed justly; for we are receiving the due reward of our deeds; but this man has done nothing wrong" (Luke 23:40-41).

We know nothing of this man who died at Jesus' side except for the little glimpse that we have of him in these awful moments on Calvary. Whoever he was, he saw two things very clearly. For one, he recognized that he was a sinner; indeed, he apparently felt that he was an unusually wicked sinner. He saw that his life was a shambles and that he deserved the awful fate that had finally caught up with him. That in itself is a rather remarkable insight. For most criminals in his position are quick to try to justify themselves. They can find all kinds of excuses to minimize their guilt. They can go to great lengths to rationalize themselves right out from under the responsibility for their crimes. But not this man. He apparently saw very clearly that he was as guilty as could be and without excuse of any kind. That in itself marks him out as rather unusual.

The other remarkable insight that he showed that day was his recognition of the unusual significance of what was taking place on the cross next to his. He recognized that this was no ordinary execution taking place. He recognized that Jesus was no ordinary man dying for his own crimes. Somehow he understood that this was a righteous man. He evidently perceived that Jesus was precisely what he had claimed to be—the Messiah. After rebuking his sarcastic companion, he turned to Jesus in a plea born of faith, "Jesus, remember me when you come into your kingdom" (v. 42).

How much he knew about what was taking place on the cross in the center we cannot know for sure. He obviously saw it as no ordinary event. He had the inner spiritual sensitivity to be aware of the presence of God in these events. He recognized that though Jesus was dying just as he was, there was something in Jesus that held the ultimate answer to his own broken life.

Had he had some prior contact with Jesus? Had he perhaps heard him preaching and teaching? Or had he merely heard others talking about him? Perhaps he had once been a devout Jew, steeped in the messianic traditions, longing for the coming of the Savior, but at some point had turned away from the teaching of his fathers. Now, at this late moment of his life, all that he had once held dear was coming into focus as he saw what was happening to Jesus. As a matter of fact, we can only wonder about this man and how he came to utter a cry of faith to Jesus in this final moment of both of their lives. We simply don't know what chain of events brought him to this point of asking to be remembered by Jesus. We can only know that things came into focus for him at the cross.

We can only know that here was a sinner who was saved at the very gates of hell. No matter what his background had been, his last minute plea to Jesus to be remembered by him brought a welcome response. "Truly, I say to you, today you will be with me in Paradise" (Luke 23:43).

Jesus gladly accepted this last minute plea and reached out to his companion in suffering on the cross with the most precious promise that can be given a man.

Surely, no man in his right mind would purposely wait until the last possible moment of his life to reach up to God in faith in a last-minute desperation move. For, who could be sure that the circumstances of the last moment would permit such a hopeful act? But the experience of this poor fellow on the cross shows for all time that if one at death's door does make the plea of faith to God for salvation, God will graciously bless him even at that late hour.

The salvation Jesus extended to his dying companion was totally of God's free grace. Certainly this wretched man did nothing to earn or deserve it. But, then, salvation always comes like that. No one ever earns or deserves it. What can sinful humanity do to earn the favor of God? That is humanity's central problem: sinners in rebellion against God with a nature that is trying to shut God out of life. People are guilty before God and are deserving of the punishment that God has clearly warned always comes to those who invest their lives in sin.

Salvation is always the free gift of God. It is God's innermost nature to be a merciful, forgiving God. God is a God of grace and love. His grace knows no limits. God does not arbitrarily set limits to his mercy. He does not determine beforehand that he will grant forgiveness and salvation only up to a predetermined number of sins arbitrarily chosen as a limit beyond which he will not go. He does not say that one can be saved anytime prior to one's thirtieth birthday, or anytime up to thirty days before one's death. The grace of God is so rich and free that God goes on seeking the lost until life is gone. God never gives up. And God never refuses one who in faith cries out for mercy. The man on the cross next to Jesus is a prime example of that for all time.

The limitless grace of God is most clearly shown, however, by what was taking place on the cross in the center. God went as far as it is possible to go in his attempt to provide salvation when he gave his own Son as the climaxing event in his centuries-long effort to turn people from their sins. John 3:16 shall always stand at the heart of the gospel message. "For God so loved the world that he gave his only Son, that whoever believes in him should not perish but have eternal life."

What else could God do? Beyond the cross he could not go. He had entered the stream of human history, sending his own Son as one of us to share our common life and endure our lot of temptations and sorrows. Jesus had left all of the royal prerogatives which were his in heaven to become one of us. And in our sinfulness we put him on a cross with the shame and weight of our sins upon him. He endured all of this in the supreme demonstration of God's forgiving grace. There could be no stronger revelation of how much God loves us. God gave all that he had when he made this kind of sacrifice on our behalf.

The cross in the center is the strongest possible demonstration that there is no limit to the forgiving grace of God. It is no surprise at all that God gladly accepted the plea of faith from the repentant thief who was dying alongside Jesus. It would have been surprising if Jesus had not responded warmly to his plea.

That central cross on Calvary—and all that it represents in the gospel—is the central event of all history. It gives meaning to life; to history. It is the sign of God's purpose in our world. That cross demands a decision from each of us. The other two crosses alongside the cross of Jesus speak to us of the crucial importance of our response to the gospel of Jesus Christ. If God loves us enough to give his Son in death on the cross in our behalf, then we must not treat the gospel lightly. Our response to the cross in the center is a matter of life and death for us just as it was for the two criminals who were executed with Jesus on that fateful day.

There are just two options open to us as we face the cross. They are epitomized by those other two crosses. We can either reject Jesus or accept him. The gospel is not neutral. It always demands a response. We cannot be neutral. The failure to make a positive response of faith is in itself a rejection of the offer of God's forgiveness. If we refuse the hand of mercy outstretched to us when we are justly condemned in our sins, then we can only sink to our own destruction. The alternatives are just that clear and simple. One's refusal of the grace of God on a specific occasion does not mean that he might not have another chance. But who can say that he will have tomorrow in which to have another opportunity to accept the grace of God?

That central cross speaks to us with the pointed demand that we humble ourselves in repentance and faith before it to receive the free gift of God's salvation. That central cross reminds us that if we refuse the gift of God's mercy we are throwing ourselves headlong into eternal personal disaster. One cannot lightly spurn the costly love of God. He who turns his back upon the cross of Jesus Christ without surrendering to the one who died there for all of us stands in grave peril before a holy and righteous God.

There were three crosses on Calvary. One signifies man's greatest hope. It stands for his deliverance from the powers of sin and death. It stands for his hope for eternal life with God and the saints of all the ages. It stands for the offer of new life now and forever. It speaks of the overarching love of God, of his good disposition to us in all of our needs. It speaks of our heavenly Father who is willing to make the greatest possible sacrifice to reach us in mercy and love.

The cross on one side of Jesus' cross speaks to us of the tragedy of being so close to salvation and yet so far. One may be close to salvation, at Jesus' very elbow, as was this poor criminal. But just being close is not enough. There are many who have had numerous opportunities to receive the Lord into their lives, but for one reason or another have never responded to the Holy Spirit's wooing. They may have grown up in Christian homes where parents witnessed to them and earnestly prayed for them. They may have had pastors and Sunday School teachers who sought to lead them to Christ. They may have had numerous friends who witnessed to them both in word and in deed. They may have been blessed by the providential care of God in many ways, receiving blessings of all kind. But all of this is finally for naught if they do not take the step of personal faith in Jesus as Savior and Lord. They, too, could be lost at the very gates of heaven if they continue to let choice opportunities to be saved slip through their fingers.

The cross on the other side of Jesus still reminds us that salvation is open to any who will call on the name of Jesus. It still makes no difference who a man is or what his past life has been, if he will call upon the name of Jesus God will still reach out to save him. He too can hear the blessed promise of the Savior, "You will be with me in Paradise" (Luke 23:43). There are multitudes of people, scattered across nearly two thousand years since the cross of Jesus, who have found that there is saving power in the message of that central cross just as the dying thief found in his own day. Shattered lives can be put back together by the grace of God. If God's power could call his Son from the tomb of the dead, so can his power mend a broken life. If God could bring the first man to birth from a handful of dust from the earth, surely his power is also sufficient to bring a dying man to new life through the new birth.

There were three crosses at Calvary, each with its message to us. The one in the center—Jesus' cross—is the one that towers over time and beckons to men with the invitation of God to life eternal. It is either the guarantee of your hope or the seal of your doom, depending upon your reaction to it.

A classmate of mine when I was a seminary student shared a rather dramatic story of her life. She grew up the hard way, in rather difficult circumstances. She did not attend church much when she was growing up. In fact, she had little Christian influence upon her during the years before she reached adulthood. She had a hard time in life. Few things seemed to be going right for her when she did reach adulthood. In fact, she succeeded in making a pretty sorry mess out of her life. She finally reached the point where she became convinced that her life was hopeless, even though she was only in her early twenties. She saw no way out of the trouble that she was in.

One New Year's Day, she was walking along the boardwalk in Atlantic City, New Jersey. It was a cold, gloomy day that only added to the misery of her lonely, tormented mind. She decided that it was time to end it all. There was no use going on in such hopeless misery. She left the boardwalk and started wading out into the cold surf to drown herself. The cold water was almost more than she could bear, but the thought of turning back was even more painful. She just couldn't face life anymore. First she was waist-deep in the water, next shoulder-deep, and then she disappeared beneath the water's surface. She struggled to fill her lungs with water and end it quickly. Consciousness quickly faded from her.

But she didn't die. The next thing she knew she was on the sandy beach with a few people quietly watching as a rescue squad gave her artificial respiration, trying to revive her. Her first thought was that she could not even succeed in trying to kill herself.

Later that night she was walking the streets of Atlantic City, still haunted by her shattered life. She walked past a little white clapboard church building. She saw the little building was lighted and she heard joyous music coming from inside. For the first time in a long time, she had the urge to attend a church service. She went inside and quietly sat down on the back row. She listened intently to the happy singing, trying to join in occasionally. She listened intently to the happy testimonies of several people who spoke of the blessings that God had poured out on them. Finally, she heard a message about the love of God revealed in the cross of Jesus Christ. Before the evening was over, she timidly sought out the pastor for personal conversation. Under his careful counsel she confessed her sins to God and opened her life in faith to Jesus Christ as the Lord of her life.

She left that little church house a new woman. She didn't have immediate answers to all of the problems with which she had been wrestling. But she was a new person—and she had a new Friend who could help her face the problems one by one. With God's grace her life began to unfold like a rosebud, gradually bringing forth radiance and beauty. She enrolled in college and then in seminary, in preparation for spending her life in vocational Christian service helping others know her Lord who wouldn't let her end it all in the surf off Atlantic City Beach on a cold New Year's Day.

The cross in the center was crucial to her. She, like the dying thief, found the blessing of God there.

8
The Cross: God's Love for You

"But God shows his love for us in that while we were yet sinners Christ died for us" (Rom. 5:8). So the sacred Scriptures tell us of the cross.

Sometimes the cross seems rather remote, a long way from us. We take it so dispassionately, as a matter of fact. We are accustomed to singing about it in church, seeing it on the church steeple, or the front of the pulpit. Some wear a delicate golden cross as a necklace or lapel pin. Such symbolism may hide as much as it reveals. Obviously, those who use the symbol of the cross in their jewelry and church architecture, and so forth, mean to bear witness to the eternal love of God which put Jesus on the cross. But such use of the cross hides the grim reality of the crude, cruel, rugged cross. It hides the awfulness of the sacrificial death of Jesus Christ. We are prone, after two thousand years of distance from the cross, to take the cross as a mere symbol of God's love to us. But the original event of the cross was far too dramatic, too awful, to be a mere symbol. We need to see it in something of its original setting. Only then can we properly relate to the cross.

Our two thousand years' separation from the cross need not keep us from seeing the cross in something of its original setting. The New Testament pretty well sets the stage for us. With only a little imagination we can visualize the cross and the events immediately preceding it. To see the cross in proper perspective, you need to see it against the background of the humble scene of Jesus' birth. The Son of God went through the deepest possible humiliation in coming to save us. Remember that he was the eternal Son of God who shared in the creation of the heavens and the earth. He participated in flinging the stars into the heavens. It was his power that kindled the sun and hung the moon in its orbit. He shared in scooping together the dust of the earth to make the first man. His power kept the universe running in proper order. As Son of God, at the right hand of the Father in heaven, he regularly received the praise and adoration of the choirs of angels.

All of this Jesus gave up in order to be born in a borrowed stable behind a tiny inn in Bethlehem. He had to lay aside the power that was his when he shaped worlds and created man. He had to give up all of the glory that was his as he sat at the right hand of God. For he was to be poured into the limits of a tiny, helpless baby. Though he was conceived in his virgin mother's womb by the overshadowing presence of God's Holy Spirit, people of his day probably considered him illegitimate. They did not know of the miraculous event of his conception, and they could not have understood it even if they had. Not until after the resurrection, some thirty years later, did even those closest to him really understand who he was.

It is hard for us to realize the depth of the humiliation he underwent in order to save us. He gave up all his prerogatives as the Son of God and truly became one of us. To say that he stooped to our level is a magnificent understatement of what really happened.

Not only did he give up heaven and all of its glory with the privileges and powers that were his, he came to save a people who rejected him. As the Scripture writer says, "He came to his own home and his own people received him not" (John 1:11). But not only was he refused by the very people he came to save, he was put to shame by those same people. They mocked him, cursed him, accused him of being the very opposite of what he really was, and put him to inhuman suffering before merciful death came to claim him. His birth in human form was humiliation enough, Almighty God poured into the limits of human life, and then the degradation of death on a cross at the hands of a frenzied mob was added to emphasize the humiliation of God's Son.

Jesus' death was no accident, however. Nor was it a surprise. It was a part of the plan of God for his incarnate life. At a critical point in his ministry, when the disciples had begun to realize that he was God's Messiah, he began to teach that he would go to Jerusalem to die. As we now look back at the life of Jesus, we can see that there was the shadow of a cross falling on him from early in his ministry, if not from the very beginning of his life. His disciples tried to persuade him to turn aside from thoughts of death—they were seemingly ready to defend him with the sword, if necessary, but he rebuked them and pushed on toward a date with destiny on the cross. It was this that he had come to do; to give his life as a ransom for many (Mark 10:45). He seemed to view his death on the cross as the crowning achievement of his life, that which he was appointed to do.

Move into the very shadow of the cross with Jesus, into those fateful last few days before the cross. He was warmly acclaimed by many as a king when he rode into Jerusalem on the back of a borrowed donkey. But few knew what kind of king he had come to be, and fewer still knew the pathway that he would take, by way of a cross, in order to sit upon his throne at the right hand of the Father once more. Many shouted at his entrance into Jerusalem. More would shout, and in a far different tone, in just a few days as he was leaving Jerusalem with a cross on his back, heading for Skull Hill, Golgotha, to give his life in cruel suffering as a ransom for lost sinners.

Jesus earnestly desired to celebrate the Passover observance with his disciples one last time. Passover was very closely related to what he had come to do in his own life. Passover was the ancient observance, instituted at the time of the deliverance of the Jews from the four hundred-year Egyptian captivity. The Passover observance reminded the Jews annually of the night of deliverance when the death angel of the Lord passed over Egypt. The death angel took the firstborn of every household except the Jewish households where the blood of a sacrificial lamb had been smeared on the door posts. It was this last act of judgment upon the Egyptians which finally produced Pharaoh's consent for Moses to depart with the children of Israel. The Jews had solemnly observed this memorial of deliverance each year since their Egyptian captivity had ended.

Jesus wanted to observe this Passover with his disciples one more time. And this time marked the end of the Passover observance, so far as he was concerned. On this occasion Jesus instituted a new memorial of deliverance. This ceremony would mark a greater deliverance than the deliverance out of captivity in Egypt.

This new memorial would proclaim deliverance out of the bondage of sin. When the customary Passover observance was completed, Jesus took a loaf of bread from the table. Breaking it before their eyes, he said to them that the breaking of the bread symbolizes the breaking of his own body for them. "This is my body, which is [broken] for you. Do this in remembrance of me" (1 Cor. 11:24). Then he distributed the broken bread to them with the command to eat it. Perhaps they were reminded of the earlier saying of Jesus, "I am the living bread which came down from heaven; if anyone eats of this bread, he will live for ever; and the bread which I shall give for the life of the world is my flesh" (John 6:51). This saying was deeply resented by some of the Jews and caused Jesus to lose some of his popularity.

In the same manner Jesus took wine, pouring it in their presence, saying that the pouring of the wine symbolizes the shedding of his blood for them. "This is my blood of the covenant, which is poured out for many" (Mark 14:24). Then he commanded each of them to drink from it. Perhaps they were reminded again of the earlier saying of Jesus, which they had not really understood at the time, "Truly, truly, I say to you, unless you eat the flesh of the Son of man and drink his blood, you have no life in you; he who eats my flesh and drinks my blood has eternal life, and I will raise him up at the last day. For my flesh is food indeed, and my blood is drink indeed. He who eats my flesh and drinks my blood abides in me, and I in him" (John 6:53-56).

Here, in the seclusion of the upper room, Jesus instituted a vivid ceremony to remind his disciples of all of the ages to come of the sacrifice that he was making for their salvation. "Do this . . . in remembrance of me. For as often as you eat this bread and drink the cup, you proclaim the Lord's death until he comes" (1 Cor. 11:25-26). What a vivid reminder of the cross and the unbelievable sacrifice made there for us! Each time the church observes the Lord's Supper, as it came to be known, it is taken back through the years of time to stand again at the foot of the cross to be reminded once more how costly its salvation is.

As Jesus observed this Lord's Supper with his disciples, the shadow of the cross was deepening over him moment by moment. And he knew it. Immediately after this deeply significant moment with the disciples in the upper room, Jesus took his little band of followers to the garden of Gethsemane, a quiet spot which they apparently frequented for prayer. Jesus was feeling the burden of his impending suffering and death. He needed to pour out his soul in prayer to his heavenly Father. He needed additional strength to bear the ordeal through which he was to pass in the next few hours. If he had not felt the weight of the awful burden that he was bearing, he would not have been human. And he was human, fully human. His humanity was as real as his deity. It was only natural that he felt compelled by the awesome ordeal just ahead of him to go to the garden and pour out his soul before God.

When he came to Gethsemane, he left all but three of his disciples at the outer edge of the garden. He took only Peter, James, and John with him into the interior of the garden where he went to pray. Here, he left these three beloved disciples and went a little farther. He knelt to pray, and prayed the kind of agonizing prayer which the world has not seen, perhaps, either before or since.

Though he prayed in agony that he might be delivered from the suffering and death that seemed inevitable, he nevertheless committed himself to the will of his Father. "My Father, if it be possible, let this cup pass from me; nevertheless, not as I will, but as thou wilt" (Matt. 26:39). After he had prayed thus for an hour, he returned to the three disciples who had accompanied him into the interior of the garden. Alas, they were asleep! He roused them and continued in his prayer vigil. His prayer was so intense that he perspired profusely: "And his sweat was as it were great drops of blood falling down to the ground" (Luke 22:44, KJV). But still the three sleepy disciples could not stay awake to pray with him. After a second hour of prayer, Jesus found them asleep again. Once more he awakened them and returned to his soul-searching prayer.

The three hours of intense prayer in the garden of Gethsemane did not open to him a way out of the suffering and death on the cross. But it did bring him that last reassurance of the will of the Father for him. It did bring him the necessary strength and courage to face the bitter ordeal that would start unfolding in just a little while.

Before Jesus and his disciples could leave the garden where he had prayed, Judas, one of his personally selected twelve, stepped out of the shadows to betray him into the hands of the waiting Temple guards. How ironic it was! One of his own inner circle betrayed him with, of all things, *a kiss* and a greeting of saccharine respect. And with that armed soldiers seized Jesus as though he had been a common, dangerous criminal. Peter, who couldn't stay awake in the garden, was now fully awake. He drew his sword, ready to defend Jesus to the last and lopped off the ear of one of the servants of the high priest. But Jesus rebuked him for his impetuous action. Then he healed the astonished man whom Peter had wounded.

From this point on things began to move swiftly toward the cross. Jesus was led through the mockery of six illegal trials—all illegal by the standards of that day. No credible charges were ever laid against him. Indeed, bribed witnesses had to be used to have any accusation at all. And even then, the charges were so ludicrous that Jesus did not dignify his accusers with so much as a single word of self-defense.

The six trials were more of a sideshow than an exercise in justice. During some of these trials, Jesus was treated shamefully. He was mocked. He was beaten. He was cursed. The shame heaped upon him in those sad hours was indescribable. Still, even as they nailed him to the cross a few hours later, Jesus begged, "Father, forgive them; for they know not what they do" (Luke 23:34).

Even as he hung on the cross he continued to endure ridicule. The people about the cross hurled insults at him and mocked him. " 'You who would destroy the temple and build it in three days, save yourself! If you are the Son of God, come down from the cross.' So also the chief priests, with the scribes and elders, mocked him, saying, 'He saved others; he cannot save himself' " (Matt. 27:40-42).

As he hung on the cross, enduring untold agony, he took the full sting of death in his body. He refused the drugged wine offered to him to ease his pain. He was bearing the cruelest kind of suffering, weighted down with the sins of the world. He was enduring the shame and scorn poured upon him by the crowd which was little more than a lynch mob. Still, his thoughts were upon others. He had already asked forgiveness for those crucifying him. As one of the thieves crucified at his side cried to him in repentance Jesus made him a precious promise: "Truly, I say to you, today you will be with me in Paradise" (Luke 23:43). Seeing his mother in the crowd, he entrusted her to the care of John, his beloved disciple.

Perhaps that cross was the loneliest spot of torment any person ever knew. Though Jesus knew that he had come to that moment to do the Father's will, the intense agony of the cross made it seem to him, even if only briefly, that even God his Father had forsaken him. He cried, "My God, my God, why hast thou forsaken me?" (Matt. 27:46). In truth, God had not forsaken him. The agony of his suffering, and the loneliness of the cross he occupied in the midst of a raving, jeering mob, made it seem that he was entirely forsaken—even by his heavenly Father. Even Jesus knew better, for in just a little while, as he breathed his last gasp of air, he said with firm conviction, "Father, into thy hands I commit my spirit" (Luke 23:46). And with this cry, the agony of the cross was over.

God's own Son had taken into himself the worst that death could do to a man. And he had broken the power of death, as would be obvious three days later when he was raised to new life by the power of God. No, God had not turned his back on Jesus. God was right there with him. As Paul would later declare, "In Christ God was reconciling the world to himself" (2 Cor. 5:19). God had turned his back on Jesus; there never was a time when God had been nearer.

Why did all of this happen? Why did God send his Son to suffer such shame and agony at the hands of sinful men? The answer lies in the limitless love of God. The cross is the supreme revelation of the love of God. But it is more than a mere revelation of God. It is a very positive expression of love—a dramatic action of love. The cross is God's way of saving man from the consequences of sin. The cross is God's way of stepping into the awful human situation to take upon himself the suffering and destruction that we were piling up for ourselves.

Although he was created by God and for God, man stands in rebellion against God. He has defiled his relationship to the heavenly Father—*he has sinned.* Modern man may not like that ancient word *sin,* but there is no other term that really fits man's situation. People have broken their relation to their Creator through defiance and disobedience. They have become a law unto themselves in the ultimate expression of selfishness. People have pushed God out of their lives in countless ways. The Bible calls this by a black name, sin. And we have all committed sin. No one has been exempted from the infection of sin. Isaiah wailed, "All we like sheep have gone astray; we have turned everyone to his own way" (Isa. 53:6). In the New Testament, Paul reaffirmed another Old Testament passage, "There is none righteous, no, not one . . . . There is none that seeketh after God" (Rom. 3:10-11, KJV). He goes on to trace the wickedness of men for several verses and finally concludes, "For all have sinned, and come short of the glory of God" (v. 23, KJV). What a sorry picture!

The picture gets even worse. Not only have we sinned against a holy and righteous God, we have put ourselves under judgment, liable to the penalty for sin. We have cut ourselves off from the blessing of God by turning our backs upon him. And it is not that people did not know better. From the very beginning of human experience God has sought to impress upon people the consequences of sin: "The soul that sins shall die" (Ezek. 18:4). In the Garden of Eden, God told Adam and Eve that if they disobeyed his commandment to them they would surely die. Paul summed it up in the New Testament, saying simply, "For the wages of sin is death" (Rom. 6:23). The fate of the sinful is graphically illustrated by Jesus in the parable of the rich man and Lazarus. Here, the rich man, who had lived very selfishly amid all his blessings, lost all that he had had when he left this life to go into indescribable torment as punishment for his sin. When people sin, they call down upon themselves the inevitable consequences of sin: judgment and punishment. By their sins they catapult themselves into the open jaws of death. And they have no one to blame but themselves.

With death closing in upon us, God sprang into action to save us from our self-imposed destruction. He gave his Son to dwell among us in order that he might point us clearly to a loving heavenly Father who wants to forgive us our sins. Jesus taught that God is a redeeming God. He demonstrated that God will go to any length necessary to save man from his sins. He even went to the cross as the supreme revelation of God's earnest desire to save man from his fate. In a sense, Jesus became our substitute on the cross. The cross graphically represents the judgment that should have been yours and mine. But he bore it for us. What Jesus did upon that cross has a vital impact upon us. Not only did he suffer punishment for us—punishment which he did not deserve—but what he did on that cross results in a change in us, if we will but accept the gift that God offers us through the cross. "God was in Christ, reconciling the world unto himself, not imputing their trespasses unto them . . . . For he hath made him to be sin for us, who knew no sin; that we might be made the righteousness of God in him" (2 Cor. 5:19,21, KJV). In the poetic language of Isaiah, "He was wounded for our transgressions, he was bruised for our iniquities: the chastisement of our peace was upon him; and with his stripes we are healed" (Isa. 53:5, KJV).

The death of Jesus Christ upon the cross and his resurrection three days later spell the defeat of the alien powers that held us in bondage. They form the heart of the gospel proclamation that God is willing not only to forgive us our sins but will also give us new life through Jesus Christ. The same power that called Jesus from the tomb is now available to rescue us from death and create us anew.

Although God has tried to communicate his love to us in many ways, the cross is his supreme effort to reveal his love. Nothing more profound can be said about God than that he loves with an infinite love and is willing to forgive even those who have sinned against him. The cross is the greatest possible demonstration of that love. When God said it through the cross, there was nothing left to be said. All the servants of God can do now is point to the cross as the final word of God in revealing his love.

It is the nature of God to love with a self-sacrificing kind of love. God is not a vengeful God who seeks to throw his disobedient children into everlasting torment. He is not an angry God just looking for an occasion to vent his wrath on some poor soul. Such characterizations of God have nothing to do with the God and Father of our Lord Jesus Christ. God is the Almighty Father who sent his Son, Jesus, to rescue us when we were not worth rescuing. No one had to persuade him to save us, least of all Jesus. Jesus came as the supreme indication that God *wants* to save us. As Paul put it, "But God shows his love for us in that while we were yet sinners Christ died for us" (Rom. 5:8).

This seeking love, seeking to save any and all that it possibly can, is the inmost nature of God. It is this love that accounts for the awful agony endured by Jesus on the cross. This was God's greatest attempt to gain the attention of man and move him to repentance and salvation. Jesus taught that God is a God of love, always seeking the lost and needy. Jesus used three striking stories to illustrate the nature of God. He told the parable of the lost sheep, saying there once was a shepherd who had a hundred sheep. One night as he put them in the fold for the night, he found that only ninety-nine were accounted for. So, he left the ninety-nine that were safely enclosed for the night and went back out into the wilderness in search of the one lost sheep. He likened God to the shepherd who would not rest until the lost sheep was found and he had brought it safely home with rejoicing.

Jesus also likened God to a woman who had ten coins. One day she discovered that one of the coins was lost. She lit a candle, swept the house, and searched diligently until the one lost coin had been found. When she found it, she called in her neighbors to rejoice with her over her finding the one lost coin.

A third story was the famous parable of the prodigal son. This was a simple story about a young man who had selfishly demanded his part of his inheritance-to-be and went off to live life in his own way. Soon riotous living had taken its toll and he found himself penniless, living in the pasture with the hogs he was hired to keep, nearly starving. When he finally came to his senses, he went home to beg his father to take him in as one of his slaves. The conclusion of the story was that an anxious father was happy to receive his wayward son, not as a slave, but as a deeply loved son upon whom he would bestow rich blessings.

This is the nature of God. He cannot rest as long as there is one lost person. It is his nature to search until *every* last one has been brought safely home, if that be possible. He will make whatever sacrifice is necessary in order to save lost men. And that sacrifice included the ultimate sacrifice—the sacrifice of his own Son living among us, receiving abuse, shame, scorn, and suffering for being one of us. That sacrifice included a pitiful death on the cross in order that he might take in his own body what we deserved for ourselves. All of this was for us, because God loves us with a love that simply is beyond description. "Greater love has no man than this, that a man lay down his life for his friends" (John 15:13).

What is your reaction to that cross? What does it mean to you? These really are crucial questions. More is involved than just your impressions and reactions. Your future for eternity depends upon your reaction and response to the cross.

If you place your faith in the Jesus Christ who died on the cross, you will be saved from your sins and know the blessedness of the Christian life. Jesus went all the way to the bitter end of the cross in order that he might bring you salvation. He endured all of this on your behalf to break through to you with the good news that God loves you—even to the extent of forgiving you and offering you new life. But the gift God offers you in salvation is a conditional gift. It has only one condition—but that one condition is a crucial one.

The crucial condition of your being saved is a positive response of faith to Jesus Christ as your Savior and Lord. This faith is not just an intellectual response of believing certain facts about Jesus as a historical figure. This faith is trust, a full reliance upon God, a full commitment to him. Where previously you had depended solely upon yourself, now in faith you shift the center of your life to him. You stake your life on him. Saving faith is an active quality of full trust. And it is the essential key to receiving salvation.

Saving faith requires that we become identified with the Son of God who died on the cross. "For surely you know that when we were baptized into union with Christ Jesus, we were baptized into union with his death. By our baptism, then, we were buried with him and shared his death, in order that, just as Christ was raised from death by the glorious power of the Father, so also we might live a new life" (Rom. 6:3-4, TEV). Paul put it even more strongly: "I have been put to death with Christ on his cross, so that it is no longer I who live, but it is Christ who lives in me. This life that I live now, I live by faith in the Son of God, who loved me and gave his life for me" (Gal. 2:19-20, TEV).

This vital response of faith, involving the commitment of the total person, is the necessary response to the cross—*to Jesus Christ who died on the cross*—if one expects to share in the salvation that streams from the sacrifice on the cross. "He that believeth on the Son hath everlasting life: and he that believeth not the Son shall not see life; but the wrath of God abideth on him" (John 3:36, KJV). Your response to the cross is crucial. God takes the cross in a deadly serious manner. You should too. Your refusal to accept the Christ of the cross only heaps further sorrow on the one who died in your behalf.

I do not profess to know all about how the cross is used by God to bring us salvation. The full meaning of the cross is always out beyond our finite minds. I only know that it is crucial to our salvation. And it is the supreme display of the self-sacrificing love of God for us. For God "spared not his own Son" for us (Rom. 8:32, KJV).

The very sight of that cross, the very mention of that cross ought to move you to the deepest contrition and reverence. It is said that when the monk Martin Luther came to realize for the first time what a sacrifice Jesus Christ had made for his salvation he was overcome with emotion. His fellow monks found him in his little room sobbing, "For me! For me!"

When you focus attention on the cross, it ought to hit you in a very moving way what Jesus has done for you in order to bring salvation to you. Perhaps the sacrifice that he made for you in his death on the cross is illustrated, in a tiny, human way, by the death of a woman who gave her own life in a heroic attempt to save her children from a burning house. She had just gone to a neighborhood grocery store a few blocks from home to pick up a few items that she badly needed. She had left her three children bedded down for their afternoon naps. She anticipated that she would only be gone a few minutes.

While she was away, fire broke out in the house. The old house was tinder-dry and the fire quickly engulfed the whole structure. When she turned the corner to her block, she saw her house in flames. A crowd of people had gathered around it waiting for the arrival of fire trucks. No one realized that there were three children inside. She broke through the crowd and ran into the house before anyone realized that she was even there. She groped through heavy smoke until she found the three frightened children huddled in a closet, terrified. She grabbed one by the hand, picked up another, and made her way to a window. Here she broke out the glass and handed the two children to startled onlookers. Back to the closet in the hall she went to get the last child. Gasping and choking, she carried the limp form of her last little boy to the window and handed him to safety. But by then her own body had been pretty badly burned and her lungs singed by the hot air and smoke. She collapsed before she could climb through the window herself, and was dead by the time others could get her out of the house.

As nearly any mother would have done, she gladly sacrificed herself in order to rescue her precious children. And those three children lived the rest of their lives under the realization that they were alive only because their mother had sacrificed her life for them.

So it ought to be when you look back at the cross. Jesus exchanged his life there for yours. And you now have the assurance of eternal life, if you have trusted him in faith, because he gave his life for you.

9
The Cross: Foolishness or Power?

Is the cross only an empty religious symbol, or does the gospel of a crucified Savior have transforming power? To the man who has not had a personal experience of salvation by faith in Jesus Christ, the cross may be just so much nonsense. At least that is the way the apostle Paul found it in his day as he declared, "For the word of the cross is folly to those who are perishing, but to us who are being saved it is the power of God" (1 Cor. 1:18). The idea of a crucified Savior was a stumbling block to the Jew who had anticipated a conquering political Messiah and was sheer foolishness to the Greek mind which was ever seeking higher forms of wisdom.

But what the world found to be both a stumbling block and foolish was used by God as the power to redeem and transform men who were undone in their sins. Paul declared the cross to be the wisdom of God which transcends the wisdom of the dying world. "For since, in the wisdom of God, the world did not know God through wisdom, it pleased God through the folly of what we preach to save those who believe" (1 Cor. 1:21). The King James Version of that verse makes it appear that it is by the foolishness of preaching that God is transforming the world. But that is not quite accurate. It is by the foolishness of that which is preached—the gospel of a crucified and resurrected Savior—that God is saving a lost world. The wisdom of God's approach to us with salvation through the cross goes beyond human wisdom.

Through the cross God provided salvation on man's level—*but not on man's terms.* God came to man on the human plane through the incarnation of his Son. He approached man on the level of human life, becoming one of us with Jesus Christ living out his life among us. He deliberately chose not to come to us with heavenly displays of signs and wonders such as the Jews might have desired. And he chose the way of the common person rather than the way of the sophisticate, the way of the Greek philosopher. Jesus simply came identifying himself with sinners of various sorts and taking their burdens upon himself. He so identified with us that he became our substitute in death that we might be saved from our own spiritual destruction. But this kind of salvation was not what the Jew expected, nor was it what the Greek wanted. The cross, however, was God's way of unleashing a redemptive, spiritual power into the stream of human history.

Paul's day was not the only day that has misunderstood the cross as the redemptive power of God. The cross is still foolishness to the many who have not been saved by the gospel of God's grace. Those who now view the cross as so much foolishness do so for some of the same reasons as the ancients. But the mistaken views of modern or ancient persons do not change the ultimate truth that the cross is God's way of reaching and changing sinful people with his own saving grace. The cross is not foolishness. It is the power of God, and this is clearly evident to those who have been saved.

We would do well to look at the reaction of both of these ancient groups, the Jews and the Greeks, toward the cross and examine their positions. If we can come to a clearer understanding of why certain ancient people refused to believe in the salvation offered by God, we might better understand how to approach modern people. The obvious reason why many people do not accept the gospel message that flows out from the cross is that they have never heard it. At least, it has never been clearly presented to them in a prayerful and persuasive manner. However, there are many more who have long been exposed to the gospel of salvation and have constantly turned a deaf ear towards it. It isn't the kind of salvation they are looking for, if they are looking for salvation at all. But if the word of the cross is still folly to some, to many of us it has been the saving power of God for nearly two thousand years.

Why did Paul find Jews and Greeks rejecting the word of the cross? He found them rejecting it for some of the same reasons that people reject it today.

It might seem strange that the Jews rejected the salvation being provided by God. After all, God had worked with the Jews as his

Chosen People, specially groomed and led for many hundreds of years to be the people through whom the Savior would come. They had been the vehicle of God's self-revelation. But when the moment of truth came, the Jews found that the message of a crucified Savior was a stumbling block to them. They weren't looking for that kind of Savior. Instead of the cross, an apparent sign of weakness, shame, and defeat, the Jews were seeking impressive signs (1 Cor. 1:22). In fact, that was one of the difficulties that Jesus had with the Jews all during his earthly ministry. "And the Pharisees and Sadducees came, and to test him they asked him to show them a sign from heaven" (Matt. 16:1). They had been seeing all kinds of signs of miraculous healing and startling compassion for outcasts, as foretold in Luke 4:18-21 (quoting from Isa. 61). They had seen the blind made to see, the lame made to walk, sinners transformed, and other sorts of miracles. Still they asked for "signs." Ironically, when they got the greatest possible sign, the resurrection of Jesus from the dead, they still refused to believe. It still wasn't the *kind* of sign they were seeking. Though Jesus did perform many signs and wonders in his mighty works, he steadfastly refused to play to the galleries; he refused to put on a cheap display of miracles simply to gain popular acclaim.

Why was the cross a stumbling block to the Jews? The answer lies in the kind of Messiah they were expecting. They were looking for a magnificent temporal prince who could throw off the yoke of Roman oppression and bring Israel to be a first-rate world power, indeed, the dominating power of the world. They looked for a Savior who would come with a mighty outward display of power which could meet every whim and need of the people. Indeed, the people were only too ready to seize Jesus by force and make him their king when he fed the five thousand with the five loaves and two fish (John 6:15). Who wouldn't want the kind of king who could set up this kind of a system catering to the needs of the people? And, surely, if he could feed five thousand so easily, there must be no end to the spectacular marvels that he might unleash! This was the kind of Savior the Jews wanted. No wonder the cross was a stumbling block to them. The cross would represent the loss of all they expected in a Savior.

They particularly scorned Jesus because he died on a cross.

The kind of meekness he displayed could be interpreted only as a sign of weakness. And his association with harlots and publicans could only be seen as a sign of his own ungodliness. The very fact that he was finally crucified was to the Jews a sign of God's judgment upon him. He must have been the most wicked man imaginable to have suffered such a fate. Indeed, they called him a blasphemer because he claimed to have come from God. The scorn and rejection that he found from the Jews was precisely what had been predicted hundreds of years before by the prophet Isaiah (53:3-4). Jesus was simply the wrong kind of Savior to win acceptance among the majority of the Jews.

The Jews of Jesus' day not only expected the wrong kind of Savior, they also expected the wrong kind of salvation. The self-righteousness of the Pharisees of Jesus' day did not leave room for a Savior. They found their "salvation" within themselves. By the scrupulous keeping of the law they thought they were in perfect relationship to God. But Jesus found them so tangled up in rule-keeping and hair-splitting that they were straining out gnats and swallowing camels (Matt. 23:23-24). Their self-righteous pride would not let them depend upon another for salvation. Jesus chided them more than once for failing to recognize their deep need for genuine salvation.

The ancient Jews were seeking a spectacular but superficial kind of salvation. They were looking for a dramatic public display rather than an inner spiritual transformation. They wanted a salvation that was based on sight—the recognition of great signs—rather than a salvation that was based purely upon faith. They wanted a salvation that was national and political rather than personal and moral. They wanted a salvation on purely selfish terms, a salvation that would provide just what they wanted rather than what they needed.

The ancient Jews were not the only ones looking for something selfish, superficial, and spectacular in religion. There are still many today who look for signs and wonders. They want a comfortable religion that meets their selfish whims. They are in search of some stirring emotional experience. Or, they are looking for some external manifestations, some kind of miracles or signs. They are looking for miraculous cures, speaking in tongues, and mysterious happenings that are contrary to the expected order of things. They want God to put on a special show just for them. They want a miracle-working God who doles out favors while asking nothing in return. They want religion purely on their terms.

All such seeking for spectacular signs cuts the heart right out of the Christian relationship to God. The essence of the Christian relationship to God is faith. Indeed, there is no other basis for approaching God than through faith. The author of the letter to the Hebrews underscores the necessity for faith in relating to God. "And without faith it is impossible to please him. For whoever would draw near to God must believe that he exists and that he rewards those who seek him" (Heb. 11:6).

The people who are seeking signs and wonders, whether of a crude or of a more sophisticated sort, are missing the whole point of the Christian gospel. A meaningful relationship to God in salvation comes only through faith. If one has to have spectacular displays and impressive proofs in order to believe in God, that person isn't exercising faith anyhow. One is only following that frothy display which excites one's curiosity or caters to one's personal whims. That is what the ancient Jews were trying to do. And the cross of Jesus Christ did not fit into that scheme anywhere.

But God did not come in the person of Jesus Christ to build a fickle following through spectacular displays or emotional orgies. He came to reach into the innermost recesses of the human heart and work a mighty moral, spiritual transformation in the lives of sinful men. If he had come only as a miracle worker with tantalizing signs and wonders, there would have always been the danger that another might come with a new set of wonders and woo away his following.

It was that very problem that the cross was designed to cure. Satan had already come to compete with God and had led man astray. God was now looking to transform the human soul and bind it to himself with cords that could not be severed. Through the cross he was seeking to transform human beings, putting sin to death, and with his resurrection power create men born anew. He was seeking to build a following that would not turn away after the latest fad. He was seeking to do a work that was more permanent and solid than the Rock of Gibraltar rather than a superficial work based upon cheap displays that fire the imagination or kindle the emotions.

The chief problem faced by humanity was the fact that they were sold out in sin; they were corrupted in their inmost nature by their rebellion against their creator. God was attempting through the cross to address this fundamental problem of human existence. How do you transform a rebellious, wicked human soul? It certainly would take more than spectacular displays, or popular, frothy appeals. It would take a fundamental approach to the heart of the problem: humanity's sinful, corrupted nature.

Through the cross of Jesus Christ God was clashing with sin in a head-on confrontation. Indeed, sin was put to death along with Jesus on that cross. Peter graphically described the crucified Savior, saying, "He himself bore our sins in his body on the tree, that we might die to sin and live to righteousness" (1 Pet. 2:24). Something happened on that cross that broke the power of sin and made possible the moral transformation of man.

But that wasn't what the ancient Jews were looking for. They didn't see their need of that kind of salvation. They wanted a different kind of salvation and a different kind of Savior. The cross was thus a stumbling block to them, and they had no use for a gospel based upon a crucified Savior.

However, those who were seeking signs and wonders were not the only ones who rejected the message of the cross. The Greeks also rejected the message of the cross, but for different reasons. They rejected the cross as sheer nonsense. The Greeks put a premium upon wisdom and knowledge and they could see no wisdom or knowledge connected with a message about a crucified Savior. The cross could appear to them only as folly.

The Greeks of Jesus' day produced the intelligentsia of the age. Greece had already given the world the matchless wisdom of such men as Plato and Aristotle, not to mention a host of other thinkers whose writings are still diligently studied. The ancient Greeks had excelled in literature and learning. They prided themselves on their intellectual accomplishments. There were many whose favorite pastime was seeking to follow intellectual pursuits. Paul encountered some of them at Athens. He went to the Areopagus, the favorite marketplace of ideas. Luke describes the place well for us. "Now all the Athenians and the foreigners who lived there spent their time in nothing except telling or hearing something new" (Acts 17:21). Paul won some converts there, but there were many more who laughed Paul to scorn over his message of a crucified and resurrected Savior.

It is understandable that the whole account of the incarnation of the Son of God, the death of Jesus Christ on the cross and his resurrection from the dead, seems strange from an intellectual point of view. But strange or not, Paul declared that it works! "To us who are being saved it is the power of God" (1 Cor. 1:18).

To the intellectual, the whole account of the incarnation of God's Son through the virgin birth, his sinless life, his death on behalf of sinners, and his resurrection from the grave on the third day poses serious intellectual problems. In the eyes of some intellectuals the whole thing seems to be so much fable and foolishness. The idea that the crucifixion of the Son of God could result in eternal salvation was incredible to the wisdom-loving Greek mind. They thought they knew better.

The Greeks were not concerned about eternal salvation anyhow. They believed that all souls are immortal and that when the body dies the soul automatically returns to God. If the life just lived was good enough, the soul might then dwell in the presence of God forever. If the life just concluded did not measure up, then the soul would be sent back in another reincarnation until the soul had properly freed itself from worldly ways.

Socrates, and many of the other Greeks, had taught that education was the way to bring about moral improvement in the life of man. If a man knows what is right, he will proceed to do it, just as the night follows the day. Thus, the Greeks put great emphasis on wisdom and knowledge. To them this was the key to changing men and their society. So, when Paul and other Christians came preaching salvation through the gospel wrought out through the cross of Jesus Christ, most of them laughed at the fooolishness of such nonsense.

Reason alone should indicate that one cannot be born of a virgin. Reason alone should make it clear that God would not enter into human flesh—the Greeks held that spirit and matter were moral opposites and that God could have nothing to do with anything material. Reason alone should indicate that a crucified man cannot rise from the dead. From whatever perspective chosen, the wisdom of the Greeks could find little understanding of the message of the cross. To Greek thinkers the cross was utter nonsense.

Human wisdom, however, has never been a pathway to knowing God or to salvation. Paul exclaimed, "Where is the wise man? Where is the scribe? Where is the debater of this age? Has not God made foolish the wisdom of the world? For since, in the wisdom of God, the world did not know God through wisdom, it pleased God through the folly of what we preach to save those who believe" (1 Cor. 1:20-21).

The wisdom of God transcends the wisdom of man. Isaiah had long ago pointed out the folly of man trying to find God on his own and save himself. He had said,

> Seek the Lord while he may be found,
>   Call upon him while he is near;
> let the wicked forsake his way,
>   and the unrighteous man his thoughts;
> let him return to the Lord, that he may have mercy
>   on him,
>   and to our God, for he will abundantly pardon.
> For my thoughts are not your thoughts,
>   neither are your ways my ways, says the Lord.
> For as the heavens are higher than the earth,
>   so are my ways higher than your ways
>   and my thoughts than your thoughts (Isa. 55:6-9).

Man must come to God on God's terms. He must seek him in humble faith rather than in proud wisdom. For Paul said, quoting Isaiah, "I will destroy the wisdom of the wise, and the cleverness of the clever I will thwart" (1 Cor. 1:19).

The Greeks could not truly find God in their human wisdom, not even in their best insights. They were incapable of understanding the cross and the gospel of Jesus Christ on the basis of human understanding alone. The chief problem, of course, was that they were in an unregenerate state, a state of spiritual ignorance, spiritual blindness. "The unspiritual man does not receive the gifts of the Spirit of God, for they are folly to him, and he is not able to understand them because they are spiritually discerned" (2:14). The unconverted man may not have the capacity for understanding the truth of the gospel until he has experienced the salvation which comes to those who place their faith in God.

There are some things in this world that are past our understanding. Our inability to understand them does not at all mean that they are false. For instance, it is said that according to aerodynamic studies the bumblebee could not possibly fly. But anyone who has stirred up a nest of bumblebees knows very well that they haven't yet found out they can't fly! The questions of the skeptics or the outright unbeliever do not change the truth whatsoever. As Paul said, while the Greeks were rejecting the gospel of the cross as utter folly, there were many others who were experiencing its transforming power. The gospel of the cross is the power of God to save lost men.

Indeed, the cross is the wisdom of God that calls all human wisdom to an accounting. It is the cross of Jesus Christ that stands in judgment upon all forms of unbelief. As Paul said, "God chose what is foolish in the world to shame the wise, God chose what is weak in the world to shame the strong" (1:27). God's infinite wisdom makes foolishness of man's wisdom.

This is not to say that there are not intellectual problems and questions that stand in the way of some believing, either in the ancient setting or on the modern scene. There are serious questions, probing sincerely for insight and understanding. These questions ought not be ignored or rebuffed. When they are sincerely raised, they deserve the best that Christian scholarship can do to supply adequate answers. But when the keenest Christian intellect has done all that is possible to supply adequate answers raised by the probing mind of the unbeliever, the fact still remains that only the experience of salvation itself can clear away the last traces of unbelief. No person was ever born again through an intellectual argument or the understanding of profound spiritual truth. Salvation comes only by faith in Jesus Christ who died on the cross.

Those who exercise faith in Jesus Christ, the crucified and resurrected Savior, find that the cross is the power of God to transform human lives which have been dominated by sin. One of the most powerful passages of human psychological insight anywhere in literature occurs in Romans 7:15-25. Paul said here that he found that on the one hand he knew what he wanted to do; he knew full well what was right. But the very moment he was contemplating what was right and what he ought to do, he was powerless to do the right. On the other hand, he also found that he clearly understood what was wrong. However, even though he knew what was wrong and was struggling to avoid it, he could not keep from doing the wrong. He found a war within himself: he could not do the good he desired, nor could he avoid the wrong that he abhorred. He cried out in desperation, "Wretched man that I am! Who will deliver me from this body of death?" (Rom. 7:24). He answered his own question in the very next verse as he exclaimed, "Thanks be to God through Jesus Christ our Lord" (v. 25). Paul found his answer to the human predicament of sin in Jesus Christ. Jesus, and Jesus alone, can give this salvation.

"For the word of the cross is folly to those who are perishing, but to us who are being saved it is the power of God" (1 Cor. 1:18). There is life-changing power which comes to us through Jesus Christ who made the supreme sacrifice on our behalf on the cruel cross. Though that salvation may not have been what the Jews were looking for, in terms of signs and wonders, or what the Greeks were looking for, in terms of some new extension of intellectual wisdom, still it was the power of God to change the lives of Jews and Greeks, both the common and the sophisticated people of this world.

Paul extolled the power of the gospel to change men's lives in another passage. He declared, "Therefore, if any one is in Christ, he is a new creation; the old has passed away, behold, the new has come. All this is from God, who through Christ reconciled us to himself" (2 Cor. 5:17-18). And it is only through Jesus Christ that this transforming and reconciling power comes. No other one of the great religions of the world can offer forgiveness of sin and reconciliation with God in personal relationship. No other religion can offer a cure to the problem of domination by sinful practices and impulses. No other religion can offer a power which will regenerate the decaying moral lives of men. Peter said it well when he spoke to the Jewish rulers in Jerusalem, "And there is salvation in no one else, for there is no other name under heaven given among men by which we must be saved" (Acts 4:12).

Countless millions of people across nearly two thousand years have experienced the power of God through the gospel of the cross. The cross may still be a stumbling block to some who are looking for a different kind of salvation or a different kind of Savior. The cross may still seem to be nonsense to some others who are trying to follow worldly wisdom rather than the revelation of God's love through the cross.

However, the fact that some today reject the cross on the same grounds that the ancient Greeks and Jews rejected it does not change its truth one iota. Recent surveys indicate that at least one third of adult Americans claim to have had an experience of being born again, of having been saved through the power of God symbolized by the cross.

Massed statistics may not prove much, but consider the story of just one person represented in those statistics. This story points up very well how the cross still today is the power of God unto salvation to those who humble themselves in repentance and faith before the cross of Jesus Christ.

John R. was a young man who had grown up in Houston, Texas. He had gone to church for a short while when he was a child, but had not gotten much out of it. He had not been converted. In his late teen years he ran with a group of other youth who were constantly looking for a "good time." After awhile they seemed to run out of something new and exciting to do. One night they decided to see if they could commit the perfect crime just for a thrill. They decided to hold up a liquor store on the north side of Houston. John knew where his uncle kept a pistol. John sneaked the pistol out of his uncle's house to use it in the planned holdup.

During the course of the robbery, the liquor store proprietor reached under the counter, as though he might be reaching for a gun of his own. John, almost instinctively, shot and killed the man. The four young men ran in terror at what they had done. They quickly split up and went separate ways. John didn't even wait to get his part of the loot. He quickly joined the Navy in the hope of getting as far away from the scene of the crime as he could.

John was sent to a Navy base in San Diego, California. Here he began to try to put back together the shattered pieces of his life. Meanwhile back in Houston, there were no apparent clues or leads in John's crime. In fact, the Houston Police Department had about written the case off as an unsolvable crime. Indeed, it appeared that John and his companions had committed the perfect crime.

John was walking the streets of San Diego one night, still looking for thrills and excitement. He walked past the First Baptist Church where he heard joyful singing. He discovered that a youth meeting was going on inside. Some of the music reminded him of hymns he had sung as a child in a church in Houston. He felt strangely impelled to go inside. Once inside, he joined in the service that was in progress. He heard a gospel message about the power of Jesus Christ to save. At the close of the service he responded to an invitation to accept Jesus Christ as his personal Savior.

When John was saved that night, he was truly born again, from head to toe, from inside out. He became involved in a number of activities to help him grow as a young Christian. After some weeks went by, John was on a weekend youth retreat with other Christian young people. Here John came to the realization that even though God had forgiven all his sins, including the murder in Houston, he needed to set things right with his fellowmen also.

John took leave from the Navy and started hitchhiking back to Houston where he wanted to confess his crime. As he rode with a truck driver across the desert, John shared his faith in Jesus Christ with the driver. The driver soon pulled over to the side of the road and the two of them got out to kneel in the sand where the driver prayed to receive Jesus as his Savior too.

When John got to Houston, he went immediately to a Baptist minister and told him his story. The minister in turn went with John to the district attorney to confess his crime. At first officials refused to believe John's story. But John gave them so much detail they were finally persuaded that he was telling the truth. John was placed in the Harris County Jail.

I was a high school student, a few years younger than John. I heard about John through the minister to whom he had gone. I visited with John in the jail numerous times while he was waiting for his trial. I went with the intention of lending encouragement to him. However, I always came away with a blessing for myself. For John had a keen and deep faith in God. He would often tell me of other inmates he had led to know Christ in the jail during the previous week.

The day before John's trial was to be held, I asked John what he thought the sentence would be. He paused a moment, and answered in a calm, steady voice, "It may be the electric chair." That was the usual sentence in cases of armed robbery resulting in murder during those years. John must have read the look of emotion that was welling up inside me. He quickly reassured me, "If I were on the outside now, and knew that I would get the electric chair, I would still come back and confess. If that is the way God wants me to bear my witness to him, then I am ready."

John pleaded guilty at his trial. Instead of a death sentence, however, he was given a life sentence at the state penitentiary in Huntsville, Texas. Some years passed by and I had no contact with John. Then, while I was a student in seminary, I sometimes passed through Huntsville in traveling to a weekend preaching appointment. Occasionally, I would stop by to visit with John.

One Monday morning as I was sitting in the warden's office waiting for John to be brought in for a visit (it was a special concession for the warden to let me see him outside of visiting hours) the warden said, "Reverend, I hope that they never do parole that fellow."

I was somewhat shocked, for I was right then at work trying to help John get a parole. I asked, "Why?"

I really wasn't prepared for the answer. The warden continued, "Whenever we get a hardened, incorrigible prisoner in here, we arrange to put him in John's cell. After a little while John and the other fellow will come by the office one day for John to tell me, 'Warden, this man committed his life to Jesus Christ last night.' John will pray for him and witness to him until he comes to Christ."

John won more than two hundred men to Christ in some eight or nine years while he was in the Texas State Prison. When he was paroled, he went to college, earned both a B.A. and an M.A. degree. The last time I saw him he was working on a Ph.D. in psychology. He had committed his life to working with people in a type of Christian ministry.

John is a powerful example of the truth of what Paul said, "For the word of the cross is folly to those who are perishing, but to us who are being saved it is the power of God" (1 Cor. 1:18). That powerful gospel works for any who call upon God in faith.

10
Take Up Thy Cross

What does it mean to be a Christian? Occasionally, I am asked if there is any one passage of Scripture which summarizes the central truth of the gospel of Jesus Christ. I think that the one passage which best summarizes what becoming a Christian is all about is found in Matthew 16:24-26. Here Jesus puts it all into a nutshell.

Notice how he begins this striking passage. "If any man would come after me, let him deny himself and take up his cross and follow me" (Matt. 16:24). In other words, Jesus was saying, "If any man will become a Christian, let him . . . ." Notice the *if*. Becoming a Christian depends upon an individual, personal decision.

Adam and Eve in the Garden of Eden were free to obey or disobey the command of God concerning the forbidden fruit. Though God had plainly warned them of the consequences of disobedience, they were nevertheless free to make their own choice. God did not have a leash upon Cain so that he could not kill Abel, his brother, when his jealous anger boiled up against him. When Job sat on the ash heap in desolation, God did not force him to maintain his faith. Job could very well have yielded to the temptation to curse God and die. In the beautiful story of the prodigal son told by Jesus, the prodigal youth was neither prevented from taking the wrong step in leaving home to squander his life on his own, nor was he compelled to come home in tearful repentance. In both instances he had to act upon his own choices freely made.

God does not force anyone to become a Christian. The choice is up to the individual. To be sure, God urges upon the individual the consequences of his choice. But the choice must finally be made by each individual. Each one must face the alternatives: to live according to one's own selfish desires or to live according to God's requirements. One may continue to live in selfish sinfulness, in rebellion against God, or he may choose to repent of his sin and become a Christian. The choice is his to make as he faces the alternatives.

But he must also face the consequences of those alternative possibilities. And here God wants us to know exactly what the situation is. The choice that a man makes in deciding whether or not to become a Christian is loaded with weighty consequences. Indeed, God urges upon us in the most serious possible tones the importance of making the right decision. "For whoever would save his life will lose it, and whoever loses his life for my sake will find it. For what will it profit a man if he gains the whole world and forfeits his life?" (Matt. 16:25-26).

The contrast here is between the person who selfishly holds onto his life, trying to make of it what he pleases, and the person who yields himself to the will of God, submerging their will in the will of God. When Jesus spoke of one losing "his life for my sake," he was not talking about becoming a martyr. He was talking about the kind of commitment to Christ that would cause one to forget about personal, selfish goals. Jesus was dramatically setting out the alternatives that are before the individual. A person can selfishly seek to build a life for himself only to come to the end and find that, in fact, no matter what he might have achieved—even gaining the whole world—he has in reality lost everything worth having. He has lost his own soul—he has lost himself in sin and its consequences, even while trying to build his own little selfish empire.

On the other hand, if one submits to the demands of Christ as Lord, one will find, in the final outcome, that he has gained the highest possible personal destiny—he will have achieved what life is all about and will have the blessings of God upon him. But, note that God does not force the decision either way. "If any man would come after me."

How fleeting and fickle are fame and fortune! "What shall it profit a man if he shall gain the whole world, and lose his own soul?" The words of Jesus make a dramatic impact. The choice one makes, whether to yield to the demands of God or selfishly to try to run life one's own way, carries very serious consequences. When you make the choice, you also take the consequences. If you try to run your life your own way, you will lose the best of life. If you lose yourself in God, you will find the richest possible fulfillment in life.

Becoming a Christian, however, is no light matter. Becoming a Christian is a serious matter, making heavy demands, according to the words of Jesus in Matthew 16:24. "If any man would come after me, let him deny himself and take up his cross and follow me." In one sense salvation is free. You cannot earn it or buy it. In another sense salvation is very costly: it will cost you everything in order to become a Christian. Jesus laid down very stringent demands for one who would become a Christian. He called for a self-surrender and a total commitment to himself as Lord.

"If any man would come after me, let him deny himself." Becoming a Christian begins with a choice made between self and Christ. As Jesus once prayed, "Not my will, but thine, be done" (Luke 22:42), so one who becomes a follower of Jesus must come to that point of self-surrender. Someone has put it rather poetically, there is a cross and a throne in every heart; Jesus must be put on the throne and self on the cross. As long as self is on the throne, Jesus can only be on the cross. For the Christian, Jesus *must* be put on the throne.

The Christian life must begin with repentance. Repentance is a word which means a change of direction, an about-face. It means that where once I was going in the direction of sin, now I have turned in the direction of righteousness. Where once I was going in the direction of selfishness, now I have turned toward God. Where once I was living for myself, now I am living for Christ. Repentance is a surrender to Christ, a self-denial. In World War II, when America and the Allied nations were fighting Germany and Japan, the only peace terms we would consider were unconditional surrender by the forces that were seeking to destroy freedom. That's what repentance is—unconditional surrender. Or, as Jesus demanded, self-denial.

The surrender Jesus asked for here is not merely negative. It ought to be seen in a positive context. Jesus was asking for positive commitment to his lordship, his leadership. In reality, the Christian denies himself in order to make Christ the Lord of his life. The Christian allows his will to be caught up into the will of

God so that whatever he does in his life he does under the leadership of the Spirit of God resident within him. This is no resignation from human life. This is a positive entrance into a more fulfilling life, life in a higher dimension. It was very well put by the apostle Paul, "I have been crucified with Christ; it is no longer I who live, but Christ who lives in me; and the life I now live in the flesh I live by faith in the Son of God who loved me and gave himself for me" (Gal. 2:20).

This positive idea of self-denial was beautifully illustrated to me by a family friend. He is an electronics technician whose hobby involves electronic gadgetry. He has built a large scale model of the ocean liner *Queen Mary*. It is several feet long, and is finished in intricate detail. He has fitted it with an ingenious set of electronic controls. Occasionally he takes the model ship to a nearby lake and launches it. He has a control panel with a variety of switches and dials. Once the ship is launched he begins to operate the controls from the shore. He can flip a switch and smoke will begin to come out of the smokestack. Another switch turns on the lights. With the press of a button the foghorn sounds. Another button rings a bell. A twist of a dial sets the vessel in motion. The twist of another dial controls the direction the ship moves. With each twist of a dial, or each flick of a switch, the ship responds with some appropriate action.

It is this kind of relationship that Jesus wants with the individual Christian. This is the self-denial that he wants—his divine hands on the controls of our lives so that as he whispers directions to us we respond immediately to do his will. In this way the Christian lives an exciting life as the servant of Jesus Christ, touching others with the power of God as God works through us. "If any man would come after me, let him deny himself."

There is a second demand of one who would be a Christian. It is an even stronger statement of one's responsibility to Jesus. "If any man would come after me, let him deny himself *and take up his cross.*" What did Jesus mean when he said that you are to take up your cross? The terminology of bearing the cross is rather flippantly used by some church-going people to refer to almost any kind of aggravation or nuisance they have to endure in life. I once heard a dear friend complaining about her hardships. "My husband's aged mother lives with us. She is sick and feeble. She either can't or won't do anything for herself. She can't sleep at night and calls me several times every night. No matter how hard I try to please her, I never seem to do anything right. I am so tired and discouraged that I am about to drop in my tracks. I guess this is my cross to have to bear."

Is that what Jesus meant when he said that the Christian is to take up his cross? Did he mean that one must have an aged, sick, crotchety, nagging mother-in-law to make life miserable for one? No! That is not at all what Jesus meant. What kind of cross was Jesus talking about? Was Jesus saying that anyone who wants to be his follower must become a martyr as he did? What did Jesus mean by this demand for cross-bearing?

The key is in the cross of Jesus itself. What was the cross of Jesus? Obviously, it was the instrument of his death. But, was that all that can be said about the cross of Jesus? Look a little closer. The cross of Jesus was the sign of his complete, unreserved dedication to the will of his heavenly Father. It was also the means he used to make possible the salvation of lost men. It was the symbol of his life purpose of saving men.

When Jesus asks Christians to bear a cross, he is asking that they do exactly what he did? dedicate themselves completely to the will of God. This dedication should include the willingness to suffer and die if need be. Indeed, it meant exactly that for some of the first followers of Jesus. If legend can be trusted, Peter was crucified upside down. When he was about to be executed for his faith in Jesus, his last request was that he be crucified head down, feeling that he was not worthy to die in the same manner as his Lord. It is said that Andrew preached for two days while he hung on a cross dying a slow, agonizing death. James was beheaded for his Christian faith. Philip was hanged. Nathanael was skinned alive and left to die a painful death. Thomas was crucified. Matthew was killed with a sword. John was thrown into a kettle of boiling oil but escaped to die in exile on the Isle of Patmos, the only one of the twelve apostles to die a natural death, according to the legends. So, many who first heard him say, "Take up thy cross," did follow him literally in a martyr's death. But their death was the death of a grain of wheat "dying" as it is planted only to sprout and bear an abundant harvest.

Not many of us will be asked to suffer and die in the course of our Christian service. But each of us is asked to take up his cross. That means we are to exhibit complete dedication to the will of God by *living* rather than by *dying*. That may not sound as heroic, but it may be more demanding. Many might be able to rise to the occasion in a moment of heroism, dying as a testimony to faith in Jesus Christ as Lord. That can be done and finished in a few moments. However, it may take more raw courage and commitment to exhibit our commitment to Jesus Christ by living in all circumstances in a distinctively Christian manner. For most of us, bearing the cross will mean living a life of dedicated service, giving ourselves without reserve to the will of God for our particular lives.

For Jesus, bearing the cross meant giving himself in complete dedication to the will of God. It also meant spending his life in such a way that the result would be the salvation of lost people. For us, bearing the cross may very well mean the same thing: spending our lives in such a way that we will enable others to find the love of God in the salvation offered by the gospel of Jesus Christ. The chief task of the Christian is to be a vessel bearing the grace of God to people who desperately need it. When William Carey, the great English Christian, was asked what his job was, he responded by saying that his job was to preach the gospel of Jesus Christ but he was a shoe cobbler to pay the expenses. Perhaps that is what bearing the cross means for us when Jesus says that any man who wants to become a Christian should take up his cross. His chief responsibility in life is serving as a Christian missionary in his whole life-style.

There was a third demand of Jesus for the one who wants to be a Christian. "If any man would come after me, let him deny himself and take up his cross *and follow me.*" What does he mean, "Follow me"? Many answers could be given as the various dimensions of following Jesus are explored. Surely, following him must include following him in personal Christian living. It means following him in a life-style that uniquely displays godliness and dedication to God. Jesus summons us to follow him in holiness and

consecration. "But as he who called you is holy, be holy your-
selves in all your conduct" (1 Pet. 1:15). Peter reinforced his
admonition in the very next verse by a quotation from the Old
Testament, "You shall be holy, for I am holy" (v. 16), quoting a
passage which occurs several times.

Follow him in holiness. Holiness is separation from evil of any
kind. It is also consecration, being set apart for special use. The
Christian, then, is to be separated from evil of all kinds. Even
more, he is to be reserved for special use, dedicated to the service
of God. Paul made a forceful statement of the same truth. "I
appeal to you therefore, brethren, by the mercies of God, to present your bodies as a living sacrifice, holy and acceptable to God,
which is your spiritual worship. Do not be conformed to this world
but be transformed by the renewal of your mind, that you may
prove what is the will of God, what is good and acceptable and
perfect" (Rom. 12:1-2). All of this means that the Christian is to live
a life that is distinctively different, and for a special purpose. He is
no longer living for himself but for Jesus. He is following Jesus,
and thus he seeks to avoid sinful ways and sinful habits, whether
they be the outward, so-called sins of the flesh, or the inward sins
of the spirit.

"Follow me," said Jesus. Follow him in prayer. As Jesus frequently engaged in prayer, so should the follower of Jesus. It is
through prayer that the Christian keeps in personal touch with
God, his heavenly Father, and with Jesus, his precious Savior.
Prayer keeps the Christian's heart in tune with God and forms a
channel through which God can commune with him and offer
him strength and guidance. Prayer may very well be the secret of a
radiant, vibrant Christian life.

A lovely college senior was killed in a tragic automobile accident. Her untimely death brought great shock and sorrow to many
on her college campus. She was a radiant Christian person who
had been admired and respected by all who had known her. Many
young men and women made the trip from their college campus
to her hometown for her funeral. After the funeral service, a group
of her closest friends went to her home to visit with her mother
and father. While they were in the home, one of them asked,
"What was the secret of Ellen's life? Why was she such a radiant,

happy person? What made her so distinctively different?"

Ellen's mother answered, "I think I can show you better than I can tell you. Come with me." She led them into Ellen's bedroom. She picked up a well-worn Bible from the night table by her bed. Opening its worn pages, some of them tear-stained, she said, "This was the secret of Ellen's beautiful life. She spent time every day reading her Bible and praying. She never let anything interfere with her daily devotional time. She walked with God."

Following Jesus means walking with him in personal purity. It means living in dedication to God even as he did. It means living in personal communion with God. It means adopting a life-style that bears positive witness to the transforming power of Jesus Christ wherever one goes, whatever one does. But it means even more.

It means following Jesus in positive acts of Christian service. It means becoming an instrument in the hands of God as he builds his kingdom. For some it means following Jesus, in the language of Scripture, "unto the uttermost part of the earth" (Acts 1:8, KJV). It may mean being a missionary to a remote spot halfway around the earth. It may mean being a pastor right in the town where you were born. It may mean using your job as a mechanic, or a lawyer, or a cashier, or however you earn your living, as an opportunity to bear witness for Christ right where you are. Being willing to follow Jesus means that you are willing to go wherever he might direct you and serve him in whatever way he might direct.

One Sunday evening, as a pastor and his wife turned into the driveway of their church, they noticed a little nine- or ten-year-old girl sitting on the front steps of the church with her suitcase beside her. Fearing that she might be running away from home, the pastor's wife quickly went to the front of the church and sat down on the steps beside her. Gently, she began to inquire if anything were wrong. Unable to discover if there really were a problem, she finally asked directly, "Are you running away from home?" She got a somewhat surprised "Why, no!" in return. So then she asked, "Why did you bring your suitcase to church with you tonight?"

In remarkable childlike simplicity, the little girl responded that since the pastor had preached that very morning on following Jesus wherever he leads, she was ready to go.

Perhaps in her immaturity she had not really understood what the pastor was saying or what Jesus meant when he demanded that the Christian "take up his cross and follow me." But you do have to admire her unreserved faith and willingness. Maybe she had not quite understood, but maybe she had understood a little better than many of the rest of us! For many of us who claim to be Christians are living as though we were totally unaware that there are serious responsibilities that each Christian is expected to bear.

Jesus said, "If any man would come after me, let him deny himself and take up his cross and follow me." What does it really mean? Perhaps it is better explained by a simple story than by pages and pages of interpretation and analysis.

A pretty college freshman was in her first weekend on the campus of a large state school. She was both lonely and excited as she was moving into college life. She hoped to be a drama major and have a career on the stage. At least that's what her daddy wanted her to do. And she usually tried to please her daddy, for she was the apple of his eye.

On that first weekend at college, some of her new friends invited her to go to church with them. She told them no, for she had never been to church in her life except for weddings and funerals. She had a little bit of a hard time telling them no, however, for they seemed pretty insistent. She didn't know it, but they began to pray for her. Near the end of the next week, some of them again invited her to go to church on Sunday. This time she said yes, almost to her own surprise.

She found herself interested in the discussion in a Sunday School class. She was somewhat stirred by the worship service. In fact, she eagerly accepted the invitation to go again the next Sunday. As the weeks rolled by, she joined the Sunday School class and began to study the Bible. She found a whole new world opening up to her. She really had had no previous exposure to the Christian message.

Shortly after the Christmas holidays she made a profession of faith in Jesus Christ as her Savior and Lord. She was baptized and joined the church. From this point on her life began to change very significantly. She was growing as a young Christian. However, she faced a crisis when time came for spring holidays. She knew that if she went home she would have to tell her parents that she had become a Christian, and she wasn't ready to face the reaction she knew that would bring.

A friend provided a way out of the crisis. She invited her to go home with her for the holidays. Since it was much nearer than to her own home, it seemed logical for her to go with her friend. So, she wrote to her parents and told them that she would not be coming home for the few days of holidays but would spend them with her new friend instead. Her parents were disappointed, obviously, but they were happy that their daughter was making good friends at school. Anyway, it wouldn't be long until school would be out for the summer and she would be home for three months.

The spring semester came to an end quickly. Now the time had come when she could no longer avoid facing her parents with the testimony of her conversion. But by now she was ready. She arrived home late at night, too late to stay up and visit. The next morning she and her parents had a leisurely breakfast together. They sat around the breakfast table, sipping a last cup of coffee, and catching up on all of the news of what had happened during the year.

During a lull in the conversation, she found her opportunity to tell her mother and daddy what had happened to her. She began, "Mother, Daddy, this year at college has been the most wonderful year of my life." They were all ears, eager to listen to their precious daughter tell of her happy year at college. She continued, "It has been the most wonderful year of my life because I have found something that I had been missing, something that made life complete for me. I have come to realize what life is really all about. I started going to church soon after I got to college. During the year I decided to become a Christian. I have taken Jesus Christ as my Lord and Savior and have committed my life to him."

Her father, who was a big man, jumped up from the table, red in the face. He shook his finger across the table at his lovely daughter, then banged his fist on the table, shouting, "You either forget that silly business about being a Christian, or get out of this house!"

She was stunned, but not really surprised. She well knew that her father was antagonistic toward the church, toward Christianity.

Quietly, slowly, without a word, she arose from the table and went upstairs to her bedroom. She picked up her suitcase which she had not yet had time to unpack. She brought it downstairs and set it down by the front door. She slid on to the piano bench and began to play and sing. She was singing her testimony from the depths of her heart.

> Jesus, I my cross have taken,
>   All to leave, and follow Thee;
> Destitute, despised, forsaken,
>   Thou, from hence, my all shalt be;
> Perish ev'ry fond ambition,
>   All I've sought or hoped or known;
> Yet how rich is my condition:
>   God and heaven are still my own!

> —HENRY F. LYTE

With that, she arose from the piano, picked up her waiting suitcase, ready to leave home, family, everything she had.

She had heard Jesus say, "If any man would come after me, let him deny himself and take up his cross and follow me." And she was showing that she knew what it meant.